JOYCE'S WAR

VOICES FROM HISTORY

JOYCE'S WAR

THE SECOND WORLD WAR JOURNAL OF A QUEEN ALEXANDRA NURSE

JOYCE FFOULKES PARRY

EDITED BY RHIANNON EVANS

The History Press

In memory of Joyce Ffoulkes Thomas (*née* Parry)
who inspired us all.

For her grandchildren:
Catrin, Owain, Lucy and Rhianwen
and her great-grandchildren
Tom, Ella, Oscar, Felix, Osian and Inigo

First published 2015

The History Press
The Mill, Brimscombe Port
Stroud, Gloucestershire, GL5 2QG
www.thehistorypress.co.uk

British Library Cataloguing in Publication Data.
A catalogue record for this book is available from the British Library.

ISBN 978 0 7509 6230 8

Illustrations © Siân Bailey, 2015

Typesetting and origination by The History Press
Printed in Great Britain

CONTENTS

ACKNOWLEDGEMENTS

With thanks to my sister Siân Bailey for her advice and support at all stages of this journey; to my brothers Ifor and Vaughan Davies, Peter Bailey and Graham McLean for their help, in particular for reading and commenting on the manuscript at its various stages and for helping to select and scan photos. Thanks also to Margaret Carleton at Edge Hill University who turned the early draft into a professional document.

Many thanks to Peter Bailey for the map illustration and Siân for the line drawings which so perfectly capture the mood of the journal.

I would also like to thank the editors at The History Press: Cate Ludlow for her enthusiasm from the beginning and Naomi Reynolds for her helpful advice and comments throughout.

INTRODUCTION

> I do want you to know that, whatever success I may attain and
> I have a cold, driving and ruthless ambition to make something
> of my life, I shall attribute it largely to you, because you, of all
> people, gave me something fresh and loyal and enduring.

The letter from which this extract is taken was received in
January 1946; the war was over and Joyce Davies (*née* Parry)
had been married for two years. She was living in Wales and I,
the first of her four children, was a toddler. We will never know
now the identity of its author but let's call him Major X. He is
not mentioned in Joyce's journals and we do not know whether
he ever received a reply because almost all of the hundreds of
letters that Joyce and her family and friends exchanged during
the war have disappeared. But we do know that it was written
in response to a letter received from her at the end of 1945
and so we must assume that Major X was as significant a part
of Joyce's war as she was of his. He may have been a patient,
a colleague or the young Medical Officer Pozner, the poet she
refers to who was dispatched to the jungle in September 1942.
This is one of the mysteries that lie at the heart of this journal

and it points to the challenges in transcribing material many years after the person has died: you cannot ask the critical questions and you cannot check the names of friends, lovers or colleagues who may be recorded only by first name, surnames or nicknames. All of them will, in any case, almost certainly be dead. Joyce herself died in 1992, and, although the family was aware of the journal, it was not until I retired in 2009 that I set myself the task of transcribing the two blue vellum foolscap volumes which had lain with photograph albums and associated papers from the war in a deep drawer in the cupboard of her bedroom.

There are many published war journals of the great and famous but there are relatively few by women, and even fewer by nurses, whose contributions must sometimes seem invisible to the generations that have no direct links with the Second World War. Nursing or nurses are not listed in the index of Anthony Beevor's recent and definitive *The Second World War*,[1] despite the critical role that they played. A few individual diaries of nurses' wartime experiences have been published, although some are now out of print, and there are also edited composite accounts drawing on the letters and diaries of nurses on active service in the Middle East.

Joyce's War tells a unique story of a Queen Alexandra (QA) nurse who set out to make a record of the war, of her experiences and of the places she visited; in so doing and unintentionally she reveals a great deal about herself. In telling her own story she tells the story of countless other nurses who worked during their formative years on active service far away from home.

Joyce Ffoulkes Parry, the oldest of six children, was born in 1908 in Caerwys, a village in North Wales, and in 1911 at the age of 2 she emigrated with her parents and her baby brother Glyn to Australia. Her father had been appointed as a minister to a Presbyterian church, where he was required to preach sermons in English and Welsh. The family settled in a manse at Ballarat, which had become a thriving town made popular by the gold rush in 1850 and where 2,000 Welsh people were living. Four more children were born: Mona, Ifor, Clwyd and Wyn, but in the years that followed the family experienced great sadness with the loss of Wyn as a baby and the tragic drowning of Ifor aged 16. His death haunted Joyce all her life and we see in the journal her particular sensitivity to some of the very young wounded soldiers. The manse was a cultured and bookish household and Joyce won a scholarship as a boarder to Clarendon Ladies' College, near Melbourne, where she excelled in English and history, winning all the major school prizes in her final years. Aged 18, after Highers, she began training to be a teacher but, following a row with her authoritarian father about her desire to read English at Melbourne University (where she had been awarded a partial scholarship), she undertook three years' training as a nurse at Geelong Hospital, hoping it would lead to opportunities to travel. Upon registration she took up private nursing posts, including one with Major-General Robert Williams, who wrote to her throughout the war. The General, as he is referred to in the journal, was a well-known Australian military figure who had been a prominent editor and director of Australian newspapers.

With a romantic attachment to Wales, the country of her birth, Joyce sailed on HMS *Mongolia* back to Wales in February 1937. There she took up nursing posts and explored with her friend Mali and cousin Gwen the Welsh landscapes 'of my beloved hills' that she recalls with such longing when she is thousands of miles away. Following the declaration of war she registered in March 1940 as a QA Sister, which was an officer rank in the army. This gave her the opportunity she had longed for to travel as well as to make a useful contribution to the war; and also to write.

Her 75,000-word journal begins when she was 31, with a month in the summer of 1940 in France (the phoney war), supposedly en route to Palestine, and ends when she is 35, in February 1944, in India on the eve of sailing back to Wales to begin her married life. In those four intense years she served on the troopship HTS *Otranto*, the hospital ship HMHS *Karapara* and in land hospitals in Alexandria and Calcutta, spending many months at sea, which led her to write in 1942: 'How heavenly to walk in a garden after so many months on a ship.' With destinations often unknown, she and her colleagues endured difficult and uncertain conditions at sea and there were frequent rumours of air raids, mines and torpedoes. Despite this, mail from family and friends from all parts of the world would arrive; sometimes there was nothing for weeks and at others a backlog of scores of letters and books.

The ships called into and spent time in ports (often for repairs) in South Africa, Iraq, India and Egypt where she records living an independent, even rather luxurious, life in grand hotels, compared to her contemporaries in England. It was certainly almost impossible before the war, or in the post-war years, for women on modest salaries to have the variety of experiences that Joyce records. She was able to go to the theatre and cinema, to indulge in shopping for clothes and shoes, or later for exquisite items for her trousseau, and she was able to stay in decent hotels while on leave. Silk or fine woollen dresses were made up from vogue patterns by tailors on the side of the road, markets were visited and ancient temples or sites were explored. There was often a party or some sightseeing with newly made friends and sometimes the social rounds were all too much and so her poetry books provided her with the solace and solitary moments that she needed to think or to write.

Throughout the journal Joyce is conscious that she is making a record of the war as she experienced it. She records with a great sweep a single day's events on 10 December 1941: 'Two days ago Japan declared war … attacked the American fleet in Pearl Harbour, Hawaii, landed troops in Borneo, the Philippines, bombed Hong Kong and Singapore, surrounded Ocean, Swains, Midway and Wake islands and succeeded in getting Thailand to capitulate – all on the first day.' She records the entry of each country into the war and charts their progress, noting the key positions of the Allies in the Middle East. With great concern she records the heavy casualties back in London or Coventry, following news on the beloved wireless. But she is also aware of what she perceives as government propaganda. After the 'grim events' of Singapore she comments: 'Apparently the government believes that the public is possessed of a very low intelligence, if it cannot see through the padding and the inane and fatuous statements uttered daily on the air and in the press.' Her own view of these events is unique: seen from heart of the action in the Middle East but always from the perspective of her twin allegiances to Great Britain and Australia, whose interests she keeps an eye on in the Pacific.

Her themes extend beyond the everyday account of living conditions on board ship, battles with the authorities about uniform, inadequate supplies for patients (they were often short of essentials) or her criticism of and frustration with the army, particularly in respect of pay: 'Nothing paid into the bank for three months and then they send it to Malaya.' She writes in great detail about the exotic places she was able to visit, capturing encounters with the local people but also moments of reflection, such as from her hospital room in the converted convent in Calcutta: 'Such a lovely morning, as I sit here writing, my windows open to the lake – full of blurred reflections, a light breeze blowing. Coolies pad up and down, barefoot, on the path below carrying stones …

a white-clad sister walks across from the wards, dazzling in the strong sunlight.' Shot through her own writing are frequent quotations from poems that she loved and her appetite for the new books and literary journals sent to her by friends and family was prodigious. In April 1941, when evacuation of the hospital in Egypt was considered, she writes that she will definitely take her *Albatross Anthology* 'in case they don't go in for poetry in German concentration camps!'

She loved India and was passionately on the side of Indian independence, which got her into trouble with many of her colleagues: 'I've been lecturing some of the boys on the ward for talking nonsense about India,' she says in December 1942. In a letter addressed from Fort William, Calcutta, in 1947, Major Ramchandani, Chief Medical Officer aboard the *Karapara*, wrote to thank her for being a loyal and staunch supporter of India and its independence.

Friendships and wartime camaraderie are a significant part of the wartime experience. Mona Stewart, who registered as a QA in London at the same time, is a constant companion and roommate up to 1942 when she is posted to Dehra Dun. Most other friends and colleagues are referred to by their surnames or forenames and in the dramatis personae I have tried to give information about some of the most frequently mentioned people. Despite her attempts to keep her feelings to herself, Joyce often writes about the frustration, the boredom and, towards the end of 1942, of her exhaustion: 'I am tired these days and my brain is weary with running or trying to run the ward with 54 patients and one orderly to help me.' While it is true that she does not allow herself much time for reflection on her personal life, her engagement is announced quite out of the blue and fourteen months later, somewhat cryptically, she records breaking it off with the words: 'Another chapter closed and another begun.'

The writing of the journal was remarkably assured: Joyce has a firm and steady hand, even while on night duty under dim light. Inevitably, because of pressure of work, there were gaps of weeks or even months but she often tries to pick up the threads in order to create continuity. Joyce did not alter one word either at the time of writing or subsequently; there are no crossings-out except for one redacted reference to a matron where the censors may have intervened and there are only two notes in the margin. It seems clear that she intended the journal to be read and we know that she re-read it after the war as there are whole pages or passages which are marked with a blue pencil or an asterisk. These are often places which are described vividly in the journal or moments which she might have to wished to recall on cold winter evenings in Swansea in the 1950s.

From a practical point of view, editing the journal has entailed the usual challenges of someone else's handwriting, wartime abbreviations and acronyms. I have transcribed word for word from the two handwritten vellum foolscap notebooks and occasionally added a word to make the sense clearer and I have made some paragraphs shorter. I have added footnotes, where I thought this helped the text; in particular I have sourced the many lines of poetry scattered through the journal. I have left her contemporary names for places she visited unless the name has changed significantly. I have added the following sections: dramatis personae; abbreviations; a map of the principal places; a postscript and index. My sister Siân Bailey has created the illustrations, which capture the mood perfectly.

Editing the journals has inevitably raised questions for me as its editor. Joyce was my mother but she was not my mother when she wrote these journals and her life then was entirely separate from the family life she later created. Is it appropriate that this former life be revealed to the world, even partially? The answer I believe is that she did intend the journal to be read as her record and eyewitness account of the war but she safeguarded herself and others by keeping aspects of her life private. Despite all the hundreds of letters exchanged between Joyce, her family and friends in Australia and Wales, and with Ken, Bob and David, sadly not one has survived. There are, however, eight letters from an envelope marked 'Letters' from other times, including from writers with whom she corresponded during the war. Her registration and call-up papers have been retained and there is also a full set of payslips together with correspondence with the War Office recording the saga of the non- or mis-payment of her salary. There are four war medals in their original box and albums containing some hundreds of photographs taken with her box camera.

Joyce comes through as a brave, loyal and independent-minded woman committed to fairness and justice, whose experiences of places, people and events are recorded vividly because she loved to write. Her dry sense of humour and her irony are refreshing: 'This morning I packed an emergency bag in case of "abandon ship" – two actually: one with essentials ... the other with as much of my new undies as I can stuff in and which I have no intention of resigning to the fishes.' Her compassion for her patients shines through together with her own modesty. She reflects on 22 May 1941:

> If by some chance I should become a war victim too ... I should hate to think my name was inscribed on a brass roll of honour – as though I were some heroine – which emphatically I am not, and should be perfectly happy knowing I had done my job according to my own standards – although they may be a little odd at times.

Rhiannon Evans
2015

MAP OF PRINCIPAL PLACES

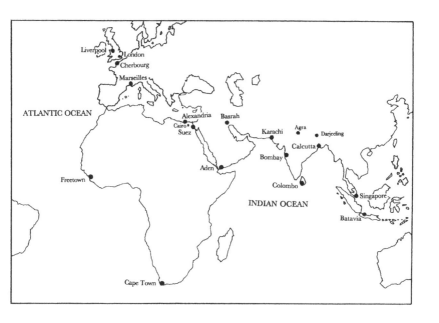

DRAMATIS PERSONAE

Many people are mentioned in the journal but below I have listed the people who are mentioned most often or where additional information has come to light. Unfortunately it has not been possible to trace many of Joyce's friends and colleagues:

Australia
Rev. Robert and Annie Ffoulkes Parry, father and mother, Ballarat, Victoria, Australia.
Glyn, brother, wife Edna and son Bruce (b. 1941).
Mona, sister.
Clwyd, brother.
Major-General Robert Ernest Williams, CMG, VD, State Commandant for Victoria and editor of the Ballarat *Courier*. Joyce was his private nurse until she left Australia to travel to the UK in 1937 and they corresponded throughout the war.
Jean Oddie and **Enid Baker**, schoolfriends who were also nursing in the ME where they met with Joyce from time to time.

Wales before the war

Gwen Roberts, first cousin and also nursing colleague in France, but Gwen elected to stay in the UK when she married Ronald.

Mali Williams, a good friend from 1937. She lived with her mother Mrs Williams and her sister Gwerfyl in *Old Meadows*, Deganwy, North Wales. Mali corresponded with Joyce throughout the war and frequently sent her books and literary journals. They remained friends after the war, corresponding frequently until Mali's death from cancer in 1951.

Ruthin, referring to second cousins Mabel and Bert, whose names are not mentioned but who lived in Ruthin, North Wales.

On board HTS *Otranto*

Mona Stewart, who registered as a QA at the same time as Joyce; they were companions, colleagues and friends throughout the war. Mona married **John Newman**. Mona also served on HMHS *Karapara*.

Bill Williams, a fellow Australian, from Adelaide, whom Joyce met in London in 1940; they were together in France and Alexandria. She married a naval captain in 1941 but died of cancer at a young age.

On board HMHS *Karapara*

Major T.C. Ramchandani, Chief Medical Officer in 1942. He was bundled off *Karapara* in 1944 on a stretcher after twenty-one days of enteritis had reduced him to a skeleton. He recovered and served the rest of the war in India and Burma. He wrote to Joyce after the war, thanking her for her support to India and independence.

And ...

Kenneth Hannan Stanley, to whom Joyce was engaged from July 1941 until September 1942. He was in 5th Indian Troop Transport Corps and in Cyprus. He married Sheila Allen, an Assistant Installation Superintendent, in December 1946 at Rawalpindi, India.

Bob, a good friend. Stationed in Basrah and possibly an army doctor.

David Herbert Davies, Joyce's first husband. Joyce married David (or Dafydd as she called him) in May 1943 at St Andrew's Church, Calcutta.

ABBREVIATIONS USED IN THE TEXT

AC1	Aircraftsman Class 1
A/C	Air Commander
ADMS	Assistant Director Medical Services
AGH	Australian General Hospital
AIF	Australian Imperial Force
AN	Australian Navy
BA	British Army
BI	British Information / Intelligence
BGH	British General Hospital
BMH	British Military Hospital
BORs	British Other Ranks
CB	Confined to Barracks
CCS	Casualty Clearing Station
CIW	Clinical Investigation Wing
CO	Commanding Officer
DDMS	Deputy Director Medical Services
DIL	Dangerously Ill List
FC	Field Cashier
HMAS	His Majesty's Australian Ship
HMT	His Majesty's Troopship

ICC   Indian Casualty Clearing Station
IGH   Indian General Hospital
IMS   Indian Medical Service
JOLs   *John O'London's*, literary magazine
ME   Middle East
MEF   Middle East Forces
MO   Medical Officer
NAAFI   Navy, Army & Air Force Institute
NYD   Not yet diagnosed
NZ   New Zealand
OMO   Orderly Medical Officer
OTC   Officers' Training Camp
PO   Principal Officer
POW   Prisoners of War
PM   Post-Mortem
QA   Queen Alexandra (nurse)
RAMC   Royal Army Medical Corps
RAMS   Royal Army Medical Services
RASC   Royal Army Service Corps
RRC   Royal Red Cross
RTO   Railway Transport Office/r
SRMO   Senior Royal Medical Officer
STO   Senior Technical Officer
TAB   Typhoid and Para-Typhoid Inoculation
QAIMNS(R)   Queen Alexandra's Imperial Military Nursing Service (Reserve)
VAD   Voluntary Aid Division
VD   Venereal Disease – now called sexually transmitted diseases/infections

JOYCE'S
WAR

1940

Wales – London – France – Troopship *Otranto* – Egypt
Cairo – Alexandria British General Hospital

August 6th 1940

*Onward bound for the Middle East
on board HMT Otranto*

At sea … somewhere north of Liverpool, the Irish coast to the left
and the Scottish to the right. We embarked on Saturday, leaving
London Euston at 6.30am, having gone to bed at 3.30am the
same morning and arisen at 4.30am. I slept most of the journey
to Liverpool. We had hopefully thought of some hours at large
in Liverpool to finish our endless shopping, but we were run
out to the docks, in the train, and then after standing with our
hand luggage on the platform for an hour or so, we were hus-
tled onto the boat – the *OTRANTO* – all set for the first stage of

adventure. After some reshuffling Mona Stewart and I are able to share a cabin together which is very small – I practically have to retire to bed to let Mona dress and vice versa. The chair and the ladder are the only moveable pieces of furniture and they have to be removed before we can turn around.

We manage somehow, however, with the two cabin trunks under the bunks and the coal scuttle which serves as a black-out – later on – under the washbasin, the surplus blankets and rugs somewhere on rafters under the roof, the cases along the lobby and the remainder where it will best fit. There is so far no water in the cabin so we have to trek upstairs to the 'ladies' where there are neat rows of washbasins and plenty of cold water but no hot water, nor will there be, we are told, for the duration of the voyage. This is very sad because we shall have to do our washing in cold water. We can have hot sea water baths but no fresh water hot baths. At present the scene in the bathroom morning and evening is a fair replica of any Grecian frieze: beauty in varying stages of unadornment, a new angle of the QAIMNS(R)[2] but hardly for publication!

Monday. We left under cover at 10pm and were allowed on deck to see the sights. It was dark, or nearly so; the English coast to the right as we went upstream, and the coast of my beloved Wales on the left. The dim outline of ships, in irregular procession – 12 we were told – several destroyers in front of us and behind us, and a torpedo last, painted in black with seven white stripes like a zebra, and probably other protecting craft that one can't see. In any case we retire to bed feeling quite safe and think no more at all that we are on the sea, and that there is a war on, and that we are involved. This morning the usual boat drill and a conference about what we may do or not do. And now I am at long last attempting to write a resume of what has happened since I joined up, or rather was called up last March. For this I need to go back a few months.

March 19th 1940

I leave 31 Prince's Drive, Colwyn Bay,[3] for the last time I think. Cousin Gwen nobly comes up to London with me. We fearfully approach Millbank[4] and I go up to be medically examined. This is a very cursory business and I am passed fit. I am given a sheet of paper on which is an address of my billet, 92 Cromwell Road, SW7. It conveys nothing to me at this time but I become extremely well acquainted with it as the months pass. Gwen and I go to Emlyn Williams' *The Light of Heart* and enjoyed it thoroughly. The next night we see Edith Evans in *Cousin Muriel* and afterwards I see Gwen off at Euston. A dreary spot to farewell anyone, at midnight, among the debris and boxes that always seem to collect there. As it happened it had to be done all over again, some weeks later, but that is another story.

The following five weeks were almost entirely given over to shopping and fitting and altering. Harrods saw us almost every day and must have been as tired of us as we were of them at the end of it all. There were bi-weekly visits to Millbank[5], to report, but in all that time we had nothing definite to do. There were theatres of course and Sadlers Wells – ballet and opera and the Old Vic with Gielgud in *King Lear.*

April 28th 1940

We left London for Waterloo and Southampton and went on board at once, but anchored off the Isle of Wight in rather thick fog until we picked up a convoy sometime after midnight. We went to bed on bare mattresses and used our own military blankets and a rug. Next morning found us nearing the French coast and we got into Cherbourg about 10am. This was our first introduction to a real war atmosphere. Many thousands of troops were disembarking, all very cheerful, khaki predominately as to colour, except for a smattering of grey and red, twelve QAIMNS(R) and all – we hoped – bound east. We toured the town, not a very big one, with the usual market square. We even had our coiffures done, which was a treat, considering how little English the French knew and how little French we knew and remembered. We had lunch and dinner at the Casino – omelettes for both meals and the most delicious French bread and butter. We got on our train about 10pm, satisfied that we were actively on the last stages of our journey to Palestine.

But it was not to be so – we were told at about 6pm that we must detrain at Le Mans and remain there about 24 hours, possibly more, as Mussolini had just made a speech which boded ill for the future action of Italy. We left the train at 6.30am and, climbing into a very high motor lorry, we were driven some miles into the town of Le Mans, which was fairly large, with a lovely cathedral and rather nice square with pleasant gardens. We were taken to the best hotel – De Paris – and given coffee and croissants and allotted bedrooms. Bill Williams, my Australian colleague, and I found ourselves on the fourth floor and fell into bed thankfully, sleeping soundly. We soon heard rumours that our stay would be more lengthy than we first thought.[6]

The weather is perfect, warm and sunny, and the gardens are colourful with laburnum and wisteria and hawthorn blossom and the chestnut trees are ablaze with thousands of candles. We go shopping, buying always unnecessary things as one does in a strange town; we walk out into the country along the quiet roads, passing villagers, farmers and the bright French children who often air their English by greeting us with good morning or afternoon. We are delighted and in turn try out our rusty French on them, often with doubtful success. We managed to procure some cider at one place and drink it at leisure under the chestnut trees in the garden while the flowers drop down into our glasses. We visit the various churches, some of them very old and partially restored. There was one, most lovely, L'Eglise de la Visitation, in the square, quite small and very light inside. We sometimes went in and just sat there, for the peace of it all. Mona and I had a delightful day at Beaumont, about 30 kilometres out of Le Mans. It was just a village with a river and the inevitable bridges, but the sun was shining and we lay in the lush grass on the riverbank and ate our lunch, which consisted of croissant and camembert, gateaux and beer, nothing else liquid being attainable locally. Mona sketched the bridge and the water wheel in the summer afternoon and I read aloud from my anthology called *Peace*: quite a lovely peaceful day. Then the ride back to Le Mans, along the straight poplar lined road, with the apple trees in blossom in the fields and the hawthorn and lilies fragrant in the cottage gardens.

Tours was another memorable day. We set off like sardines in a tin, in tiny third-class carriages, with country folk and French hoi polloi and babies tightly jammed together. I stood most of the way and watched the countryside pass by, the eternal poplars and quiet winding roads, sometimes the bed of a river, a chateau – all rather reminiscent of our last summer's holiday. Then Tours – a large, well set out town with fine buildings. We did ourselves well at lunch at Hotel de l'Univers. Then to the cathedral: 12th century, very fine indeed, with two bell towers. We climbed one tower, over 300 steps, and surveyed the surrounding countryside: the Loire a broad full stream spanned by several bridges, the country rather flat but beautifully green. Chestnuts in flower wherever we looked. We crossed the river later and poked about the old quarter of the town which was most interesting. We went back to Le Mans in the golden evening and, as we approached the town, we saw the large aerodrome floodlit, which struck us as strange when everything was supposed to be blacked out.

Everywhere we went we found some change because of the war – patisseries and gateaux were only sold on three days of the week; meat, spirits and cider on other days.

We were allowed Ff35 messing allowance per day, but this didn't cover our meals. We rarely had breakfast and often had lunch or dinner in our rooms. This usually consisted of rolls or croissant and butter and cheese, followed by gateaux or fruit and assisted by cider or some light wine such as burgundy. The occasional meal, which came to about Ff20, we had at the De Paris or Grubères in the square, or latterly at the Moderne. A fortnight passed pleasantly enough, in this fashion, and after many rumours, we had orders to depart in a fortnight. We set out for the station some miles out of town – a siding really – in the closed ambulance. We were two to a carriage affair and fairly comfortable. We were on our way to Marseilles and Palestine – as we hoped this time. It was a delightful journey south and very leisurely. We took two days and two nights, passing through large towns and tiny villages. Tours, Peret-le-Morial and Bourges.

We crawled into Marseilles after an early breakfast – and were taken into the town by bus with our hand luggage and billeted at the hotel Louvre de la Paix, a very superb hotel in the Canabière. We had very pleasant bedrooms and for a while we lived in very luxurious surroundings. The meals were quite nice in the grand French manner; however I got rather tired of them in the last two days – too rich I suppose. We visited Notre Dame, with its superb view over the harbour and town. Palais Longchamps was rather fine – built by Louis Napoleon (I think), that period anyway. St Victor Abbey was most lovely. Part of it dated back BC and was, we were told, the site of a pagan temple. Political prisoners were kept in the underground crypts during the time of the revolution. Small French children were being taught their catechisms in the church itself, with one eye on us and one on the benign old priest.

At the end of the week we had orders to pack up once again and return to England. Since we had arrived in France, Norway had fallen and later Holland and Belgium. The Germans were actually on French soil in the north and the situation, according to what we could glean from translations of the French newspapers, was 'confused'. Something had apparently gone wrong and we were heading back to England.[7] It was not so comfortable on the return journey, four to the carriage instead of two – Williams, Stewart, Walker and I. We tried lying down the first night but reconsidered it the second night and sat up instead. The carriages were fearfully congested and we were all in a thoroughly bad temper with ourselves and everyone else. The meals on the train consisted of bully beef done in various ways – fried for breakfast; stewed for dinner and in sandwiches for supper. The cooks, ordinary Tommies who had probably never boiled an egg in ordinary life, did nobly in the circumstances and usually we did full justice to their efforts.

We pulled into Cherbourg about 10am. How different it was now, from when we left it only a month before. It was a quiet undefended port before, now there were troops everywhere, ammunition dumps, bombs, guns, barbed-wire entanglements, planes in the sky, and ships in the bay. We were taken in a bus under guard to the Casino for breakfast. Everyone looked so sad and subdued – they had seemed so happy before when we passed through on our way south. We ate nearly cold omelettes and coffee and departed for the ship. There were crowds on the wharf: troops, refugees, two QAs, Dutch soldiers; luggage going up at either end, the endless tramp of marching feet, buzzing of planes, army lorries coming and going, endless activity. This went on for probably three hours and then we were underway, with dirty lifebelts strapped under our chins. We had lunch and I went to bed in order to get rid of the headache accumulated over two days of train travelling.

When I awoke we were nearly at Southampton. I am told we were chased by submarines and that we had a spy on board and would not be allowed ashore until morning. It is rather disgusting to be so near England and to have to remain on board. We went through customs in the morning, duly, and were told that we are to go on leave until we hear from the War Office. This piece of news suits us all admirably. I ask Mona to come with me to Wales, and so it is arranged. So strange and unreal to be on the train bound for London again when, only four weeks ago, we felt we had left it for the duration of the war. Mona had sent a wire to her friends to tell them that we were coming. We had our heavy luggage sent to 92 Cromwell Road as of old and, very weary and dirty, we stayed with friends at number 18, where we came in for a good deal of ragging about our frustrated attempts at going east! This was Saturday and on Monday we left for Wales. I had rung Miss John and Mali previously and Mali had insisted on our staying with them in Deganwy. Lovely to be setting off for Cymru once again; I decide to do what I have long meant to do since I first arrived – climb Snowdon. We had ten lovely days in Wales, most of them spent with the Williamses in Deganwy, but we managed to have two days in Ruthin at the end with my cousins Mabel and Bert.

I shan't write any details here except that we climbed Snowdon – Mali, Gwerfyl, Mona and I – and saw that enchanting panorama of hills and lakes and valleys at our feet, in unforgettable grandeur. We went to Bodnant one afternoon which was most lovely with azaleas, rhododendrons, laburnum and wisteria – all at their best. One day in Ruthin stood out – Mona and I left early, taking lunch with us, walked up the Bwlch and over the hills towards Llanarmon. We lay there for hours; it was so entirely remote and peaceful. The Vale of Clwyd will always remain one of the loveliest spots on earth to me. Then there were two visits to Port Meirion, one with Gwen and Mona on a wet and dreary afternoon and the other in blazing sunshine, the tide in, and then a mad dash through the mountains, Aberglaslyn, Llyn Cwellyn, Beddgelert, in the too glorious evening to catch the bus to Caernarfon. But this is another story ...

June 5th 1940

We are bound for London once again, having had orders to report to Millbank. The orders infer that we shall be leaving very shortly for the Middle East. We hastily re-pack our trunks and then as the days and weeks go by, we gradually have almost everything out of them again and, because it is so hot in London and we are so tired of wearing our grey suits, we thankfully get back into mufti again. Nothing very interesting occurs as war continues sporadically; we find ourselves down in the front hall one night, as the result of an air raid signal, but not again. There are the usual theatres: *The Tempest*, very beautifully done at the Old Vic, and some more opera and ballet at Sadlers Wells.

The predominating feeling of all these weeks is lack of pay, which continues despite our efforts at composing missives to the paymaster, in turn cajoling, pleading, and threatening. We are at last given two months' pay, and that pacifies us temporarily, but this soon goes and we get restive and sit down and write again to the paymaster. Before further combined and rather seething communications, the gentleman is moved to pay £11/7/- into my account. No one has any idea why as he owes me quite £7 in allowances. It became increasingly intriguing to us to consider how their minds work. Everyone is paid a different sum – when they are paid at all – and for no apparent reason, as we are all supposed to be either sisters or staff nurses. So it goes on, week after week. Our views on the War Office are unprintable. We occasionally agree and condescend to have tea with some misguided soul who thinks she is doing her bit for her country by entertaining his Majesty's overseas troops and nurses. Once we rose so high as to have tea with the Countess of Clarendon and another day with the Duchess of Devonshire, which was all very illuminating one way or another. Mostly the other. All this time no letters from home at all (14 weeks). I hear through Auntie Clara that Mother has been very ill and is in hospital and so I send a cable to ask how she is and am very relieved to hear in about three days that she is almost better. With deadly monotony we report bi-weekly at Millbank, say, 'Yes Matron' when she calls our names and as quickly depart. We repeatedly hear rumours that we shall be going soon but ten weeks go by before anything does eventuate and then it is the same rush all over again, repacking and half the things we meant to do and buy, remain undone.

August 12th 1940

So now we pick up the threads from the start of this journal after a brief recap. I am writing on deck, on the port side, a lovely breezy morning. The sea is a deep blue, inclined to silver where the sun strikes the waves. The other ships of the convoy seem scarcely to be moving at all, but they stay with us faithfully. The only cruiser left with us goes nobly on ahead. One afternoon – I was sleeping in my cabin – before the other cruisers and destroyers left us, there was a great deal of excitement about a suspected submarine. It seems one destroyer suddenly dashed off, full steam ahead, and then dropped several depth charges. This is the only excitement so far, fortunately. The officers gave a dance on Saturday night and invited the nurses. I went to bed instead – it was too sticky inside. There was a church service yesterday afternoon. The troops stood outside in the blazing sun and listened most politely – as far as one could tell – to one of the worst sermons I've ever listened to. Blah! Last night there was a concert afterwards and community singing; usually the Scots element predominates at these functions because there are so many Scots on board – Scots Guards, Black Watch and so on.

I leaned over the rails and watched the moonlight on the wake of the ship, gilding the waves to gold, the other ships like great phantoms gliding nonchalantly besides us. A strange sort of war indeed. This is as much like a pleasure cruise as any ship's company could provide: sports on the boat deck, tennis, quoits and all the rest. We are allowed to wear mufti after lunch until dinner. The crew and the men are all in tropical kit today and look terribly cool and clean. Even the chairs in the dining room have the white covers on them. We have been having a far from polite discussion about whether we shall wear our tricolenes[8] as mess dress or our white overalls. We stuck out for the tricolenes as the white drills will be so hard to launder. Also we have won our point, although whether it is worth it or not remains to be seen.

The sergeants – who look more interesting than the officers – have invited us to a dance this evening.

August 17th 1940

Land again – Freetown, Sierra Leone. Mona and I have been sewing and ironing all day and by the late afternoon we realise that the ship's engines are slowing down and that we must be in port or as near to it as we are permitted to be. We go up to the boat deck and a lovely sight greets us: a smallish scattered town nestling on a green hillside with rugged mountains beyond and banks of low white clouds in the blue sky. Ships and craft of all sizes and description are lying idly in the bay. It is unbearably hot, however, and memories of the Australian summer at its worst rush back to me.

We are given quinine tablets because of the outbreak of yellow fever in Freetown. Also, after much alteration and labour generally we don our white overalls for dinner, as a gesture. It is lovely on the boat deck after dinner with a cool breeze blowing, for which we are truly thankful. This morning I awake to the cries of the local inhabitants below, endeavouring to sell their wares: bananas, coloured baskets, handkerchiefs and the like. Now and then they burst into song – *The Lambeth Walk* and other equally inappropriate ditties. They are not supposed to come alongside because of the fever and, to get rid of them, they are headed off with the fire hose. They look so colourful with their sleek black bodies and close cropped heads in their bark canoes. Without more ado than getting in and out of bed they leave their canoes and dive in after any sixpences that might drift that way. On the starboard side there is a curious looking tanker with a Chinese crew from which we are taking oil. Boat drills this morning, a new station again: number six.

The news seems to be increasingly grave at home and in the east. Surely this will be a long war or else we will come out of it very badly.

August 19th 1940

Life on the ocean wave once again. We left Freetown about 8am yesterday. Mona and I had got ourselves out of bed with a supreme effort at 6am and 6.30 saw us leaning over the port side, B deck. We had our best entertainment by the local inhabitants, who dived and sang to us and kept us thoroughly amused. One comedian came dressed complete with top hat and collar and tie, doffed his hat before he dived for sixpences and returned as immaculate, except for a slightly soggy collar and a tie that hung damply over one shoulder. He gave a delightful impression of a Salvation Army preacher – in short he would have brought the house down in any theatre.

So we watched the palm-girt shore slip slowly back into the distance and disappear, and now we are heading for Cape Town, around the 'bump' and rushing it, as we are to be in port in a week's time, so it is said. In the meantime it is hot, so hot that one feels one cannot possibly go on day after day, wet and sticky and exhausted with it all. The cabins are the bête noir of the trip – we dread going down there to dress and iron. By dinner time Mona and I feel at enmity with all our fellow creatures. Daily we meet at 12.45pm for a passion fruit parade with John and Woody – an institution no less, and then again before dinner and for coffee afterwards. We have endeavoured to appropriate a table and chairs in the annex where it is cooler and less frequented. It rained last night, suddenly and stormily, and cleared again as quickly. And today it was lovely on the boat deck: very fresh and breezy except that I had washed my hair in the morning and it blew everywhere in the wildest confusion.

August 31st 1940

Cape Town is a memory – and we sail on – no-one knows where. Ten days of sea between Freetown and Cape Town. The usual routine – boat drill, sometimes an emergency one, when things are done more realistically, the boats lowered, the whole crew assembling on deck and we are turning round putting up shutters and then sitting on the floor until the four bells sound, sending us to our boat stations.

For some time the sergeants were most social, inviting the sisters to dances – Monday night at 8, whist drives and concerts but for some reason these entertainments have been cut out – we think the officers have intervened for reasons best known to them. The officers hold a dance each Saturday evening and one night last week there was a concert, various topical sketches and songs on A Deck. We sat in easy chairs and toyed with shandies when the occasion demanded. Afterwards, going out on deck we saw a hospital ship quite near us, brilliantly lit, in green and white and red lights – a strange and lovely sight – in these blackout nights. Then there was the usual last minute rush to write letters – about nine this time – and nothing to put in any of them, and then getting someone to censor them. Mona got John N. to do hers and John W. did mine – so it's all an endless farce really. And so to Cape Town, ships in the bay and Table Mountain rising sheer and stark above the town, a cloudless sky, warm sunshine and the town lying before us.

Mona and I were on duty in outpatients on Tuesday and Wednesday – the day we reached Cape Town – but we finished up early and after lunch walked into town. We meant to do a lot of shopping but leaving under pressure, arranged to meet the boys at 3.30pm and to have tea with them, we got little enough done in the end. The town itself isn't very large and the shopping is distinctly expensive. Elizabeth Arden creams at 4/6 in England were 10/- and so on. But there are many fine buildings, tall and straight in the modern style, often with friezes in stone around the walls, or over doorways; heads of famous African chiefs or sometimes Dutch motifs. We had tea at the Waldorf, very noisy and modern and American, and afterwards, by taxi, went along the rim of the mountain and along the sea front to Camp Bay, which is a very lovely stretch of coast, quite rocky in parts with the waves thundering in spray on the headlands. We got out of the car and scrambled onto the rocks. It was lovely beyond words to stand there: the sea surging around us, the long stretches of very white fine sand, the red roofed houses among dark green pines on the hillside, the sun beginning to set over the rim of the sea, making a golden path across to our feet and the mountains standing firm behind us, touched with a rosy light – all so lovely. I think we could have wept easily enough – all four of us. These are things that remain; even wars seem fleeting and unimportant in comparison. A golden evening.

We went then to the Del Monica, a new looking café, very large and somewhat bizarre, and where it seemed all the army and the navy and the QAs had decided to eat, or more particularly, to drink. It was in the Moorish style with midnight blue sky and artificial stars waxing and waning, *comme il faut*. We had some exotic cocktails, choosing them for the poetical worth of their names – Alhambra, Angel's Kiss, Blue Moon, and Orange Blossom – and then went upstairs to eat. White-turbaned Indians waited on us and we dined, if not wisely, very well. We celebrated something – I don't remember what – with champagne and wine, very happy to forget much that was better forgotten for the moment. We went somewhere else after that and eventually arrived back at the ship, by taxi, about 11pm. It was enchanting for us to see lights once again, by night, having lived through months of total darkness and walking around lightless decks every night on board. It seemed too wonderful to be true that the streets were brilliantly lit and that windows of houses and cafés poured forth a steady warm glow and that neon lights winked unrestrained against the sky. We went up on a deck for a few minutes to watch the hillside under the mountain, a veritable diamond necklace against the dark sky. Next morning, up betimes and after wasting some precious hours, we eventually got into town by bus. We started on a shopping campaign but got very little done in the end, although I did manage to get a cable to the family to say that all was well. It seems as though I shall never see their familiar handwriting on an envelope again. By this time the matron in Haifa must be almost snowed up with our steadily accumulating mail.

We came back to the ship for lunch and as we were setting off for town again, with the boys, someone asked us if we were going into town and said, if so, that he would drive us. Before we knew what was happening it was arranged that his wife would drive all four of us up Table Mountain, or as far as one could go by car. After a considerable time at the cable station, awaiting our turn for the funicular, we eventually all packed in and in seven and a half minutes were transported to the very top of Table Mountain. Gradually, and miraculously, the panorama unfolded itself as we ascended and the smaller hills dwindled, and Lions Head looked like a perfect coconut pyramid – the tall pines below began to shrink and look like shrubs, the sea shimmered like silk, under the blue sky, and the boats, far away indeed, were no bigger than canoes.

Once there, the top of Table Mountain presented an enormous rock garden on a grand scale, small rock flowers and shrubs sheltered under the great boulders. To stand on the edge gave one, alternately, a sense of power and weakness – to be monarch of all one surveyed and to be a mere dab on the horizon. Away, some forty miles, rose the Drachenburg range, mysteriously shrouded in mist, with their peaks outlined jaggedly against the sky. From the terrace below the café, more hills, sheer and grim, others bathed about their feet with cloud. We had tea in the lovely little café and then started downwards again, the sun pouring richly across the sea (I couldn't see at all, without my very dark glasses). We wasted a good deal of time then, going in search of the lady's husband, who insisted on our going to his club to take the local sherry, before taking us back to the ship.

After a wash and brush up we set out again. Mona and John went to Del Monaco and John W. (who was detained to do a small job) and I went off to the Mount Nelson hotel some distance out of town. It had a superb entrance and a long palm lined drive. Inside it was like any good quiet hotel in England or Australia, except that the waiters, as seems to be normal in Cape Town, were Indians. We were really too late for dinner, it was almost 8, but John saw the head waiter and all was arranged. We started tropically with paw paw, the first since I had left Australia, and continued through turkey and trifle and fruit salad as the waiter insisted. Coffee in the lounge completed a pleasant quiet evening. It was nice to get away from the ship's crowd for a while. A taxi back to the ship and then bed about 1am.

We left Cape Town at 5pm next day. We were not allowed on shore during the day, which annoyed us considerably, as we wanted to do more shopping and there seemed no reason why we should have to stay on board. We had managed to get some fruit and flowers the previous day: lovely oranges and mandarins, guavas, passion fruit and apples. The flowers were a sheer joy: heather and proteas, anemones, ranunculus, freesias and Icelandic poppies in gorgeous profusion. We have some now on our table and I like not to think that they will shortly die. We are in the first convoy now heading east and then north. There are a goodly number of ships, more than before, and larger ships including the *Empress of Britain*, the *Empress of Canada* and the *Shetland*. The *Ormande*, we have left behind it seems, as she is too slow for us.

It is getting hot and muggy again, and we like it not. This 'organised waste of time' as John calls it, continues, in spite of determined efforts to combat it. I do nothing all day and go to bed quite exhausted with the effort. We do open our port hole, having unofficial permission from the steward as we have no light showing through from the corridor and it is safe enough, and even so, the cabin is unbearably hot and airless. Tropical kit tomorrow – into our tricolenes and white drills once again. It is said that we shall arrive at our destination in 16 days and without any more ports of call.

I shall be most thankful when we are really established at last, wherever that may be, so that I can unpack and really spread myself out once more. If it is a tent, I'm done for once again. It is Sunday morning, no boat drill and everyone is sitting around in odd groups, writing, playing chess or cards, or just sitting, as I propose to do, even now.

September 6th 1940

Calm seas, blue skies, warm breezes, and gorgeous sunsets – the Indian Ocean as I remember it in 1937. The sky was perfectly lovely the night before last. The sea at one stage was a heavenly blue and the sky a pastel pink, where it met the sea on the horizon, with delicate opalescent clouds suspended just above the horizon. The sea was so still we could see the reflection of the *Empress of Britain* as she rode alongside us and the smoke from the funnels of the other ships hanging in the air in a black horizontal line halfway between sea and sky. From the port side later, the sea was a delicate turquoise, the ships standing out in a black relief against the setting sun, setting really like a great lantern and sending its last beams across the still waters to our ship's side.

At night, leaning over the rails on A Deck, the sky was peppered with stars, countless millions of them.

> ---- Look how the floor of heaven
> Is thick inlaid with patines of bright gold;
> There's not the smallest orb which thou beholdest,
> But in his motion like an angel sings,
> Still quiring to the young-eyed cherubims;
> Such harmony is in immortal souls;
> But whilst this muddy vesture of decay
> Doth grossly close it in, we cannot hear it.[9]

There was a moon too, yellow as cheese, coming in on its back. And the cool breeze played about us while we leaned out into the darkness, and the phosphorus, where the foam curled away from the ship, was the only light, it seemed, in the entire dark world. There was an officers' dance on Thursday night but the atmosphere became too awful after the first hour and we had to come up for air. Last night we were invited to the Sergeants' Mess for a concert. Quite a lot of unsuspected talent transpired, much more than we can manufacture in our lounge, I fear.

This morning, the news reported that over a thousand planes were over England and Wales last night. One can't imagine this somehow. The whole city was lit by parachute flares, and once again, Londoners 'dragged' their weary limbs into air raid shelters. It all seems so impossible that such things are taking place, every day and every night, when we spent so many weeks in London and it was then quite quiet and peaceful. It's rather maddening to think that we shan't know, until the end of all this and we return there, if we are still extant at such time, just what damage has been done and who has suffered.

Here on the high seas, our days are as flowing and as uncoloured as a dream. The rest of the convoy accompanies us faithfully, although they often veer off alarmingly and change places with each other for reasons least known to the commodore, who is on this ship. This morning, a light cruiser, not ours, appeared ahead of us, and cutting through the water and between our convoy, passed us in a flash, low and clean out of the water. Also we hear that the *Empress of Canada* had a fire on board this morning. Everything apparently is under control or so we hope. John has come over to sit with Mona and I have cleared off to try to finish this in peace. Mitchell is threading his way, in and out, to the accompaniment of tinkling glasses. The usual groups sit about, reading, playing cards or chess but mainly just talking. It always seems to end thus. There is a dance tonight in the enclosed part of B Deck, beyond the annex. As a special privilege we are allowed to wear evening dress and as I haven't brought a long frock with me, I am borrowing one of Bill Williams' – black and straight. It fits very well but I feel I shall look a trifle sombre, if I can't think of something to brighten it up a little. But now I must write some letters so they won't be filling up the very last day, as is usually the case.

September 8th 1940

The dance is over, and I believe we are all feeling the after effects, even at this late stage. The heat and various other things have laid most of us rather low, and no one except Mona looks really energetic. The dance was an entire success because first and foremost we were allowed to wear evening dress, and for once, we all felt and became human beings and not merely registered numbers in the QAIMNS(R).

Mona looked, as John said, 'smashing' with her hair done 'dauphin style', and in her floral black frock. I wore Williams' black frock, which fitted perfectly, and with the aid of Cameron's belt with two large crimson poppies on the front of it, and my dear cherry amber beads, I felt fairly happy. The boys had dinner with us, John having dug us out of the hot cabin with a martini. Mona had had an exhausting day, setting, out of the goodness of her heart, at least eight heads of hair, including mine. Dinner was a noisy and hilarious affair, and ended with a Grand Marnier in the lounge, followed very soon, for me, by a cup of vegemite. The dancing was practically impossible, but we got up just the same, but I was tired, tired, tired. I simply sat on the basin in the cabin, when we eventually got down, as I hadn't enough energy to undress and get into bed. Yesterday, being Sunday, we attended church parade where the singing was very good and the choir was composed of about 30 men from the ranks.

They looked so young and had such delightful faces. I always think, when I look at them, that they are being asked to give too much – to destroy and be destroyed – 'to pour out the rich sweet wine of youth'.[10] But it all seemed beyond our control just now.

The news is grim again this morning, hundreds of planes over London, fires, explosions, machine gun fire and bombs.[11] What devastation and loss of human life. Swanton has just asked me if Mona and I would be afraid in an air raid and, as I don't feel that I could ever be afraid in any situation and, in any case, one has to face such things sometime, I said, 'certainly not'. So it is arranged that Mona and I, in such an event, would take over stations in the ship's hospital to render first aid and so forth.

September 13th 1940

Hot – hot – hot. So hot my hand sticks to the paper as I write. Mona and I are sitting as near as we can get to one of the spit-fires, in our usual spot at the far end of the lounge. We have done nothing for days but sit languidly and mop our brows, or when we are not so occupied, we drink the coldest and longest drink we can persuade Mitchell to produce. The passion fruit has become exhausted, and also the orange, so now we have descended to pineapple with large lumps of ice. It pours from us almost before we have finished it and the whole thing has to be done again, in endless succession and with no lasting result.

Yesterday at about 4pm, a long convoy of ships passed us, going in the opposite direction, far away on the horizon, bound for India or Australia or elsewhere – all under escort, of course. I suppose at that time there were about 30 ships to be seen, including their escorts and ours, which consists now of two cruisers, three destroyers, HMAS *Hobart*, among them. Dinner from now on is at 6.30, instead of 7.30, and as we were leaning over the rails about 8, the *Empress of Britain* and the *Empress*

of Canada and the Andes suddenly get up speed and left us.
The Hobart came cutting through the water, between the Andes
and us, and shot out of sight in no time. We passed Aden and
Perim last night. So odd to see the lighthouse flashing out to sea –
all lights are strange sights to us now. We cluster around and look
like children at any lighted ship or beacon in these dark nights.

Yesterday morning we were told that there was air activity and
we must carry our life belts, strictly at all times. Also as Mona and
I have to take up action stations at once if there is an emergency,
we have to carry our 'shipwreck bags' and our tin helmets as well.
The men are censoring letters alongside us and reading the spicy
bits out such as, 'There are a number of nurses on board but they
are for officers only!' and 'I've never seen such a flat footed lot
of nurses in my life!'. There was some more about officers being
absolutely incompetent and having no faith in them whatsoever,
except for one or two who were worth their weight in gold and
so on. In a moment we have to attend a lecture on Palestine; it's
rather late to start this sort of thing as we are rumoured to be
arriving in Suez at dawn on Monday – and this is Friday.

September 15th 1940

More heat, day-long and night-long but these last two nights we
have had permission to sleep out. Mona was not allowed to go
up on deck because she has a bad cold, but I went and had John
Newman's bed and felt so happy to be lying under the stars
again. I believe I was too excited to sleep, but wakened many
times to find the moon staring down at me, shining silver, from
a clear starry sky. The rest of the ships glided like black etchings
in a sea of pure silver. We had to rise at 5.45 to clear the decks
for Physical Training and, leaning over the B rails from 7–8am,
I had a heart to heart talk with John N. again about Mona. It is
all arranged – they are going to be married *après la guerre* and

I am really delighted about it all. They will feel sad at heart tomorrow when John goes on his way to Khartoum and Mona – who knows where? We celebrated at dinner last night, the boys dined with us, it being guest night, and we all had a happy evening. The last deck was the scene of much horseplay, mostly by the guards, who seem to want to relax for once. We went off to bed at about 1.30am and rose before 6am.

The cruiser *Shropshire*, which has been with us since Liverpool, left us yesterday afternoon. She came close alongside, portside, and signalled 'goodbye and good luck' and her crew were plastered against the rails and up and down the rigging. All our troops collected on portside to wave them farewell and to sing 'Rule Britannia'; so much so that we have had a distinct list to port ever since. We go on alone now, making a dash for Suez, which we are supposed to reach tomorrow at dawn.

And so the final stages are reached. One more lap, by train I suppose, and we shall arrive – where and what and when is another story, of which I know nothing at this moment. I met a Welsh boy from Harlech today – rather late in the trip – such a nice lad, from Radio Telephony, who is going to Cairo. So this is the last record that I shall write here, whilst on board this ship, unless we receive orders tomorrow that we are to return to England, the same way. Even that wouldn't surprise me. I doubt if anything can in these mad days. There is talk of invasion of England today.[12] I keep wondering what is happening all day.

September 19th 1940

So this is Egypt!

But first to pick up the threads. We got into Suez at dawn on Monday morning, the hot sun blazing in the sky, the bare yellow hills, the gleam of sand beyond incredibly green water, ships lying at anchor all around us, and the engines silent after all these long weeks. After many rumours we learned that we were disembarking on Wednesday. Some of the crew got off that day, some including John W. the next day and so on until Friday. We watched them go off under their officers on curiously primitive-looking black barges pulled or pushed along by a funny little tug affair. That night after a very late dinner we had a final toast to John and he insisted on our going out on deck as a final gesture and, very solemnly and melodramatically, we threw our glasses into the sea and in a second, in a moment in time, the sea had swallowed them up in the darkness. It was a marvellous night with brilliant moonlight and the knowledge that so soon everyone must go his separate ways, not knowing whether any of us might meet again, made us sad enough to loathe going in and leaving it all. I gave John my *Oxford Book of Verse*, because he is fond of poetry too and I have other anthologies.

Mona and I went on duty the next day in the hospital. As it was the first time we had been asked to do it, apart from outpatients, we couldn't complain, although it did seem unfortunate that we were not in for the last day and had all the discharging of the men to do. John W. left the ship that morning, bound for Geneifa, some outpost in the desert, but no one seemed to know quite where. We had an exhausting day in hospital, finishing up about 5.30pm with things more or less straight, and had a party before dinner – John N. and Mona, Michael, Jackie and Andy and myself and consequently arrived at dinner very late indeed. After dinner we had another 'extra special' with Mona, John and Michael and I. We took our glasses out on deck, in the pitch darkness, for'ard, under the bridge and there we drank a toast to Mona and John, to the years between and the years afterwards that they might be together again, very soon and live happily ever after. And then we all threw our glasses into the darkness, heard the thin sound of them hitting the water below and then turned and went our ways. Later, hearing about the engagement, various people came up and joined the party: Bill and Sydney, Andy, David and Walsh, Nigel Davidson and Dr Denton and we made exceeding merry till 11.30pm. Mona went to bed then but John took me out again on deck for a deep discussion on Mona and other matters. I have solemnly promised to cherish her and look after her, until the end of the war.

Next morning, our heavy luggage having gone ahead the previous day, we had nothing to do but sit and wait for the time of our disembarkation. We left immediately after lunch, and piling into a launch with our hand cases we left the old *Otranto* and, in about 20 minutes, were in Suez. It was hot and dusty there, waiting for our cases in the midday sun, and apart from visiting the local NAAFI for a very warm lemonade, we sat in the train, tired with the heat, until we left at 4pm. It was a dreary run across the desert, nothing but sand and an occasional village, with squalid flat-roofed houses and some straggling palms. We eventually arrived at Cairo at 9pm, thankful to have arrived. The New Zealand girls were collected into a van and sent off to the NZ hospital at Helmieh and were put on duty next day. Mona, Bill and I got into the next van but, on discovering that my hand case was missing, I got out and Mona followed suit. Unfortunately Bill was left behind, and that bus went off to Helwan and the girls, except Bill, who isn't well, are now on duty. It is sheer luck that we remained behind because we are now at the Victoria Hotel, 50 of us all told, and the remainder at the Heliopolis House. The latter is more luxurious than our place, and as it is seething with QAs and their respective matrons, and we have only Fossie, and she doesn't count anyway, we feel we have the best end of the stick. The Victoria is full of Aussies, mostly on leave from Palestine. We have orders that the grey tricolenes may not be worn, and we have to order the white tricolenes to be made at once, and also to buy a white felt hat.

We have done quite a lot of sightseeing already, and have adopted a real gem of a Dragoman[13] – one Mahomet Ali el Shair. The first morning we set out on a shopping expedition and Mahomet Ali accompanied us, paying our bills, carrying our parcels, looking after us like a fussy old hen. We all climbed up into a horse-drawn gharry and went off to the bazaars. There we visited the perfume king of Cairo and bought extravagantly, perfumes to the sum of £1 for a small bottle. Mine is 'Secret of the Desert' and Mona's 'Tutankhamun'. They also gave us a little bottle of anything else we wished. Mona chose 'Wattle' and I 'Attar of Roses'. Then we went to a silk merchant's and each ordered a dressing gown and slippers to match. Mine is heavy oyster silk, embroidered in pinks and blues, in reproduction, so I am assured, of a 1713 piece of old English embroidery. Very lovely anyway. They are being made alike in Persian style and will cost £2.

In the afternoon Mahomet collected us and we set off in a taxi to visit the mosque of Hassan. We walked under the pulpit and, turning to Mecca, made a wish, this being the correct thing to do. It was a fine mosque, lofty and austere and dignified, with lovely mosaics on the walls. Then we went to the citadel, which is a fortress, to the Alabaster mosque. Surely this is the most lovely church I have ever seen – thick red Persian carpets on the floor, solid carved alabaster columns and hundreds of crystal spheres hanging from the roof. How entrancing it must have looked when the lights were lit; the sun shining in from the western windows made the crystal chandeliers miracles of beauty, and all the colours of the rainbow. There were two pulpits, one built with the mosque 120 years ago, and the other opened only a week ago by King Farouk. It was perfect, in a modern style, with gates of solid gold in an intricate pattern of leaves. All was peace and light there and we were loath to leave and go out into the hot sun again.

But we piled into the taxi once more and made for the pyramids. I have always wanted to go to the pyramids and it seemed strangely familiar to stand under their shadow in reality. The Great Pyramid took 30 years to build, ten years to quarry the stone, ten to lay the foundations and ten to finish it. There is no cement used anywhere to hold the stone together, and the men were changed every three months. We had a camel ride too, three of us, and had our photographs taken at the top with the pyramids behind us.

We went back to the hotel later for dinner but the night was yet young and at 8.30 we set off once again, two taxis this time, with Mahomet as our guiding star as before. The idea was to see the pyramids by moonlight with the dervishes and the feasting and carousing which went on all night, the occasion being a sort of thanksgiving for the cotton crop. It appeared that after the crop was harvested, all the eligible young men of the village decide to get married, and did so forthwith on the one night around much jollification and very much noise. We marshalled camels once again and a long string of us rode in the moonlight, weaving in and around the houses, watching the dervishes wailing and chanting from the Koran, small groups drinking tea, the thick sweet tea with lemon that we had drunk in the afternoon at Mahomet's house, or tiny dolls' cups of Turkish coffee.

We visited the house of one bride, a young, frightened, rather lovely girl, sitting on the roof top with her maids and her family and as many others as could squeeze in. She was awaiting the arrival of the groom, who had probably only seen her twice in his life before, and everyone was standing or sitting or dancing. He came then, the young groom, flying up the steps in his colourful robes and into the room where the young bride had been hurriedly conducted. But in a moment or two he was out again, flourishing her handkerchief high over his head in triumph, and was off to join his friends. Apparently he came to claim her permanently some time later. We had been to the houses of the bride and her bridegroom in the afternoon, and had shaken hands with them and wished them luck. As we arrived at the house of the bridegroom, the band, which was evidently hired to play to the company, somewhat strangely switched to 'God save the King', which we did recognise, fortunately, and we were quite touched. We went at length to Mahomet Ali's house again, to drink the sweet lemon tea and had our fortunes read in the sand – under the moonlight. We were tired but entirely happy as we climbed into the taxi and set off for the hotel, arriving somewhere between 1 and 2am.

Friday, September 20th 1940

We had a quiet day, much needed, and at night there was a dance given by the Australians. They were pathetically delighted that so many of us were Australians and New Zealanders and we were told that many of them had not spoken to their own womenfolk – or any English – since the war began. One persistent gentleman badly wanted me to accompany him to the zoo on Sunday, but as I didn't care for zoos and didn't care for him, I declined. Not daunted he found out the number of my room at the desk and rang me up at 1am and again when I was in the bath the next morning, since when he has been silent and, I hope, moved far away. I met quite an amiable boy from Sydney and as he had his chief's car we went for a run in the moonlight, and to the fort of the pyramids for the fourth time in two days. Home at 2.30.

On Saturday, we took Mahomet and in two cars about seven of us went out to the ancient city of Memphis and Saqqara[14] where very little remains but flat roofed dirty hovels and an enormous lime-stone figure of Rameses the Great, lying prone on great stones. On his head the crown of Upper and Lower Egypt and the false beard which was a sign of royalty. His wife is carved on his leg. It might have been done yesterday instead of 6,000 years ago. Nearby, in an enclosure, is another colossal statue of Rameses, in his heyday, with the crown of Upper Egypt only, before his later conquests. There is a belt swathed around his waist, with his name thereon and his sword in its sheath. The face is superb, with its perfect cast of features and the smile so real it was positively uncanny. A most amazing piece of work.

We packed in again and set off across the desert to Saqqara where it was desolate enough in the middle of the desert: nothing but the lone and level sands stretching far away. We descended into one of the tombs where Mera[15] was buried in the first dynasty. The mummies and the gold and such treasure which were buried with them are, of course, in the Cairo museum, now alas closed for the duration of the war, but the walls are carved with inscriptions and perfect bas relief scenes depicting the various interests of the king during his lifetime. Here fishing from a boat, Mera watching the dancing girls, Mera hunting or supervising his cooking – all this and more perfectly plain for any eye in any century to read. A good deal of the work was coloured with dye from flowers, and, except for where tourists have with their customary imbecility rubbed or scratched it away, the colour remains perfect after 4,000 years. In an alcove was a statue of Mera himself. In another apartment, Mera's wife and scenes illustrating her days covered the walls there. Across another stretch of sand we entered another tomb, the SRMO of the Egyptian court, the court doctor in fact, and there was an enormous theatre table, where apparently he got someone to sit on the patient, while he proceeded to remove something or another. Next door was a smaller tomb, the last resting place of the doctor's daughter – it seems this girl married the king's son. In the car again and down into another tomb where the colouring was marvellously fresh and clear. In another room were two mummies, rather revolting but a very amazing sight.

We started for home and then through the fertile Nile valley, the cotton crops, and the corn and the endless date palms, so cool and green against the bare yellow sands. We had dinner and Ted called in the car for me and we went for a run – first to Heliopolis and then, after various attempts to get on the road to Ismailia and being stopped at the boundary gate three times by fierce-looking Sikhs with wicked-looking rifles, we gave up and went down and sat for a while by the moonlit Nile. I fear it was exceedingly late, or should I say early, when I crawled into bed.

September 21st 1940

I didn't get up for breakfast but messed about unpacking and so on. We have space to spread ourselves in this large room now and I think I may fairly say that we are taking advantage of it. Bill comes over for lunch and we lie about or iron respectively. Mona and I have purchased a lovely little iron – universal – for 85 piastres and simply wallow in our ironing; it is such a treat to have one to ourselves. We go off to the Church of Scotland in our beautiful grey belvederes, white hat, shoes, stockings and gloves, the three of us in a gharry, and we feel like pocket Queen Victorias and look like Yeomen of the Guard. A nice little church but the padre had a dreary voice and would work his eyeballs up and down. The sermon was something about the sins of the fathers being revisited upon the children, but I dozed off before I learned the real reason for all this. Later we had dinner and Bill went back to Helmieh and I went out for a run with Ted for a time, but got back soon after 11pm. He goes out to the Battery[16] today for the rest of the week.

September 22nd 1940

Up betimes – Mona and I are sleeping in a large four-poster now with a magnificent mosquito net surrounding us – and take it in turns to see if any of our letters have arrived – but in vain. We then do a little shopping and buy some little water coloured sketches of Egypt – camels and pyramids and so on. Three of the girls overheard Matron in her doorway say that we may draw £2/10/- in advance pay, three times a month, so we shan't starve after all. We have written to the matron of the 61st general hospital, which is now in Nazareth, to ask for our letters to be sent on to us here, as Matron doesn't seem to think we are going to Palestine at the moment and we pine daily for some mail. Bill comes over and we have tea brought to us in our room and then go into town for further shopping. We have not long deposited Bill at her bus station and now I am trying vainly to get this journal up to date. I shall fall into bed any moment now …

September 23rd 1940

To the bazaars to pick up our dressing gowns and slippers and then we purchased other materials for mats and coverings for our future home or hut. I spend between 2 and 4pm ironing quite happily, and then after eating a large and luscious mango we departed to the dressmaker for a fitting of our white tricolenes. We went to the pictures and then Raffles, and, as we had had no dinner, called in at the Casino and had sandwiches and coffee followed by an ice – vanilla, chocolate and mango mixed. It was delightful sitting there on the terrace, in the cool night, with the world going by below us: cars and lorries, Egyptians, Arabs, Australians and British soldiers, and a few QAs – the whole motley crowd. After many years we shall remember the nights in Cairo – just like this. And now to bed under the mosquito netting.

We have just heard that the *City of Benares* has been sunk and all but a few of the evacuee children drowned.

September 29th 1940

On Wednesday evening Mahomet Ali hired a felucca[17] for us and we spent about one and a half hours on the Nile. These ancient boats have gone up and down the Nile unchanged for thousands of years. It was delightfully cool, scudding through the water with the starry sky above us and the palms and hibiscus lining the river banks.

On Thursday Bill came in from Helmieh, looking very worn and tired – they all loathe it out there – so preserve us from ever following suit – and may we yet land in Palestine. We went to Tommy's Bar for sandwiches and coffee instead of having dinner at the hotel.

Yesterday I had a letter from Mother re-addressed from Colwyn Bay and one from the padre whom I had befriended in London. I had a siesta after lunch and needed it – and a final warning from Flossie, the Matron-in-Chief, that we must not in any circumstances have anything to do with, what they are pleased to term in the army, 'other ranks', which means that our fellow Australians, who are not officers, we must firmly but tactfully ignore.[18] How lacking in all feeling and humanity the army is. Now we have been allocated a separate lounge where we may not be contaminated by the mere rank and file!

October 2nd 1940

The Eve of the Feast of Ramadan

Bill Williams was off today, and came over from Helmieh last night to sleep. As it happened none of us slept as it was particularly noisy without and the beds creaked unmercifully each time we turned. We did some shopping and began the process of opening our accounts in the National Bank of Egypt, Lloyds' agent there; in case the paymaster should ever think fit to send us a cheque. This seems unlikely, but it looks well to have a banking account, even though there is nothing in it.

As tonight is the beginning of Ramadan and we knew the mosques were all to be lit up, we asked Mahomet Ali to suggest something interesting for the three of us. It was decided that he should meet us at 4pm in a taxi and we would go to the Governate where we would watch the Governor of Cairo lead a procession from the law courts. This sounded interesting enough but it transpired that we were to have one of the most thrilling and picturesque evenings of our lives.

Mahomet Ali, always mindful of our welfare, spoke to the major of the Egyptian troops and got permission from him for us to go and stand on the pavement in the best possible position to see the governor emerge. It was like a scene from *The Talisman*[19] to see the long rows of white Arab horses with their superb riders and their orange and red helmets flying in the breeze. Then came the military band playing *Colonel Bogey* with great zest, followed by the infantry smartly turned out in khaki, with leather poches around their waists on which were the moon and stars of Egypt and, of course, the usual fez. The lieutenant colonel of the Cairo city police came over to us and gave Mona permission to take photos. We chatted to him and asked him numerous questions and were delighted when he told us that we could go with him to the Mohammedan Park to watch the ceremony which was about to take place there. We were given right of way through the gates and conducted to a sort of enclosure outside the law courts. The roof was open to the heaven but the walls were hung with tapestries of brilliant colours and intricate design and the floor was covered with huge Persian rugs on which there were rows and rows of chairs, some of them very ornate. While we sat there drinking out of tiny cups, delicious spiced tea, we were introduced to various notable people who wandered in and out, mostly sheiks and army officers.

Then we went outside again to watch the scene with eager eyes and scarcely believing our good fortune. The band played under the awning, the soldiers 'at ease' in front of us, groups of smartly clad officers in white and scarlet and gold chatted under the palms, flowers falling from the jacaranda tree almost at our feet, people crowding onto the flat roofed houses opposite, soft-footed servants running about putting lights up for tonight under the trees, coffee thick and sweet (Turkish), sweets, cigarettes coming around in swift procession. In between we were being presented to various officials, while press photographers took several group photographs and, it appeared, mostly of us. The patrician features of the sheiks and of the high priests as they arrived for the ceremony gave the impression that the scene was part of the Arabian Nights' entertainment and not 1940, and we were part of it all.

Bimbashi, the lieutenant colonel, was so sweet, answering all our questions in extremely good English and forgiving our extreme ignorance. He has already agreed to send the photographs to the hotel tomorrow and he asked our permission to include it in the Mohammedan magazine, with the names. He said he would send us a dozen copies of this. The important assemblage disappeared into the mosque to await the arrival of the news – by Marconi – as to where the crescent moon had been sighted, for unless it is actually seen in one country or another where Moslems are watching for it, Ramadan does not take place. The messenger arrived presently to say it had been seen at the observatory in Helwan outside Cairo so everything was alright. We went then with Bambashi up to the Citadel to await the firing of the 21 guns, announcing that Ramadan had officially begun, and to see the minarets light up, one after another all over Cairo and indeed all over Egypt, for it appears that they all wait for the Citadel to light first before following suit. We were the only ones there, it being a fortress closed to the public after sunset, and it was a thrilling sight to be high above the city and to see Cairo at our feet, springing to life out of the darkness.

Into the car again, then on to an Egyptian restaurant where Bimbashi insisted on taking us to have a real Egyptian dinner. The *pièce de la resistance* was a grilled pigeon, killed and cooked whilst we waited, so we learned later, a gruesome thought, although the birds tasted delicious and we ate them, *comme il faut*, with our fingers. Bimbashi arranged that we should go with him on Friday to the Coptic and Egyptian museums and then to the University Mosque where the king was praying that day. He was getting special permissions from the ministry of works and was calling for us at 9.30. Alas, this was all cut short for on Friday we were on our way to Alexandria and our future home.

Next morning we were told not to leave the hotel as we were getting orders to move on. This upset us a little, as of course we were not ready; we never are when the time for moving arrives, and there were overalls to collect from the little Turkish dressmaker who had been doing odds and ends for us and everything we possessed had to be picked up at once. We learned later that twelve of us, and five from Heliopolis, were detailed for the 2/5th General Hospital, Alexandria and that we were to leave next day. That left us free to go to the Sezara Club with Mona, John, a sister of a friend of Mona's, and we spent a most pleasant afternoon there with her and her husband who is a captain with the forces. They were such nice people and I found in the end that both were from Wales originally. That night Mona and I took ourselves – for a last treat in Cairo – to the

Continental Savoy for dinner. This cost us 100 piastres each, so it was just as well we left Cairo the next day.

We departed in an army van at 2.30 the next day, and after a rather uninteresting run, arrived in darkness in Alexandria about 8pm. The assistant matron met us and we started on our first run to the hospital in total blackout. It was all strange: full of new sounds and sights as a new house always is. We were given supper and allocated to our bedrooms for the night. Mona and I shared one in the mess but others went down to the flats on the Corniche Road.

November 22nd 1940

It is nearly two months since I wrote this up – although I try to do it regularly. In that time we have thoroughly established ourselves, got the feel of the wards, and the mess, explored the town itself and altogether made ourselves at home. We are all very happy here, liking the matron particularly and the general atmosphere in which we are working. Mona and I, after about three weeks in the mess, have moved down to the flats on the Corniche Road where I have a corner room on the right and Mona on the left of the back flat, second floor. There is a superb outlook especially from my balcony, along the shore to Alexandria and the harbour. I can see the sunrise o' mornings and the sunset by night from my bed. We have been busy fixing up blackout curtains for the doors and windows – I have dark blue – and have also made a cover for the trunk. We have each bought a folding table which we propose to stain and which should prove to be an invaluable piece of furniture. We are mostly happy down on the Corniche and don't for a moment begrudge the walk up in the early mornings and at night. We have dragged Beatrice from her lair in the kit bag and put most of her together again, and she more or less willingly boils our water for coffee when we require it.

As for ward work – I have been on B Ground from the beginning. It has 108 beds and is Septic Surgical; an enormous ward really, one can scarcely see into the furthest corner. I was on day duty for about six weeks but am on nights now. We have at times had our full quota of patients, which makes it very heavy, but quite recently it has been made a CCS, and so we keep the men only so long as it takes them to get sorted out and then they are sent elsewhere to the 62nd Jerusalem or the 19th at Geneifa or the 8th, which is between here and Alexandria. We do however keep all naval patients as there is nowhere else for them to go. Just now we have had quite a number from the *Maine*, the hospital ship in Alexandria's harbour. They have had a noisy and nerve-wracking time down there during air raids at night and so have been sent up to us. I think they are glad to be on terra firma and in the comparative peace of it all. We have had a lot of Aussies and New Zealanders in from time to time. One day a tall lanky boy arose from his bed and said, 'Excuse me Sister, but are you Joyce Parry?' With astonishment I replied, 'I am and who are you?' Then it transpired that he was one Cecil Brown, erstwhile of Shelford, whom I last saw as a small boy at school!

The nights are long, especially as we are so slack, and trying to keep conscious between doing active jobs is as difficult for me as anything can be. There were no raids last night, for a wonder, and have been none tonight so far. The night before, my night off, there were five all told. Two of them I missed, being too deeply asleep to hear the sirens, but there were more than 40 killed and 70–80 injured and over 80 killed in the previous bad raid and 100 injured – all civilians. The raids have been bad in England again, nearly 300 killed in Coventry in one air raid alone[20] and a thousand and more casualties altogether. It is so awful to think of the desolation and the waste of life and property.

I am hearing from Mother on a regular basis now, but the English mail is irregular and slow. The only person I hear from with any regularity is the Australian padre I met in London, who apparently thinks I must be written to once a week at all costs! Bill is still at Helmieh, Cairo, and not liking it any better. She has been up to Alexandria twice – flying once – on her days off. She hopes to get a transfer here one of these days. Mona and I go to Cairo on our days off when we come off night duty, that is, if Mona is allowed to stay the extra days to coincide with the end of my month.

Greece of course is in the war now and we are vitally interested just here because we are so near to these fast moving events. A friend of Mona's, an MO who has been in Palestine for some months, has gone to Greece and so has John Brennan, the paymaster for Cairo. He rang me up the previous night, somewhere in Alexandria. He couldn't say where, but probably they were on their ship awaiting their departure. I shall hear about it later I expect. I do hope I shall get a transfer to Greece myself after I have done a few more months here as I always did want to visit Greece, and now to be so near, and yet so far! Our two prize burns cases were transferred to the 62nd today. They were so ill when they first came in, both were on intravenous drips but they are simply wonderful now. I'm really glad they've gone however, because they did demand, and got a good deal of attention.

November 23rd 1940

I had a good sleep today. Mona and I went out on a minor shopping expedition to the little Greek grocery store in the tiny village near the 'new house' on our way down to the Corniche. Coming back a very dirty but very beautiful Egyptian woman was sitting on the kerb with her two children. The smaller of them must have been no more than ten months old but she waved to us in the friendliest cheeriest way and called, 'Saida, Saida'. Well schooled these native children are, much less self conscious and much more cute than our children at the same age. Later, I decided to put permang[21] on my folding table before going to bed. I made the gesture of putting on a pair of gloves and got to work. When I took the gloves off my fingers were coal black from the nails to the knuckles. A more revolting sight you never saw. It took fifteen minutes with a pumice stone to remove the evidence. When I awoke the sun had set and the sky was smoky grey and the last vestiges of pink were slinking away. It was time to arise, and take my shower, alas cold, and to put the iron on, for the battle frocks need pressing every time one puts them on.

Good news tonight – if one can call any war news good: Koritza has fallen to the Greeks and Albania, it seems, has assisted. No raid for three nights; we hardly know ourselves. No doubt, however, we shall pay for it later on.

Athenordon, the Greek, with a hydrated cyst of the lung is my biggest worry at night, apart from Rifleman Smith who has a large plaster sore. The rest sleep like children and there is very little to be done for them apart from a few painkillers. I have just come across from C2 E, from supper – the sky, black, with a million stars and the tall tower of B Ground standing clearly against the sky. Rather a nice building, altogether, this erstwhile 'Victoria College'.

November 28th 1940

I think it must have been the night I last wrote this up that we had our worst raid so far. The sirens went at 4.45am when we really thought that everything was over until the next full moon and soon the navy was exceedingly busy with pom poms and a terrific barrage of fire and guns. One or more planes flew quite close over the hospital and it seemed a bomb was dropped less than quarter of a mile away. It must have been then that the machine guns went off. I was up at the end of the ward taking temperatures when suddenly, amid the dull thud of bombs and the muffled notes of the fleet guns, came the sharp rat, tat, tat of machine gun fire. I feel certain it was done so that it was just outside the window where I stood and I quite expected to see holes where the bullets had come through.

It transpired, however, that it was our own Lewis gun, belonging to the Army CC, which is just over the fence from Isolation. It is said that one of the Egyptians got excited and let the gun off by mistake. It seems 'gippos', as they disrespect-fully term them, are quite impossible once they get worked up and that's why they don't send any air flares up much here as so many of them have been obligingly shot down by our own guns. Whether they are so successful with every aircraft one doesn't hear. Well, as a result of this raid, four persons were killed and more than 30 injured. But the windows of the build-ing near the centre are completely shattered, and a block of flats just behind us had a direct hit, although the people were fortunately in shelters and escaped. There has been nothing since and we hope there won't be, for it is disturbing to have to put all the lights out, just as the washes are in full swing.

Life goes slowly on otherwise. The Greeks seem to advance daily, where I don't know, but everyone seems very delighted about it, so it must be in the right direction, at least. I've had odd letters during the week: two of them have drifted in from General and one from Mrs Williams, two ship mail ones from Mother and one airmail, and yesterday, a ship mail from Mali and another from General. It seems his son Bill is coming overseas, I suppose to Palestine. My sister Mona also may be making tracks this way for she has been summonsed for a personal interview and was to go very soon after she wrote.

Strange if she were to come to Palestine and even Egypt, but they say an Australian hospital is opening here very soon. There is some talk that we may have to take our leave very soon to get it over. It will be ten days and we shall certainly spend it in Palestine if we can possibly scrape up £20. It's a great life this, a month or two of work after many months of idling and then there is talk of more leave.

I had a night off last night. It is so marvellous to come off in the morning and to know that you have got two whole nights to yourself and that the ward with its smells and its worries – these in the correct order as to their importance please note – may temporarily be forgotten. I went to bed for two hours in the morning and then got up and had a scratch lunch with Mona in her room. Then into town by train for some odds and ends of shopping.

We went to an Indian antique shop and bought some rather pretty hand-blown cocktail glasses – mine were in blue and Mona's green and amber – and some glass plates and bowls to match for the flat. Very cheap too, one piasta for the smaller ones and one and a half for the larger ones. In that shop they have a piece of a mummy of a princess and goddess of ancient Egypt. It seems that she was supreme in Egypt in magic and the supernatural. The remainder of her has been left in Paris! The old Indian who owns the shop is most amusing about her, probably he repeats the same stories to customers every day year in year out but custom never seems to stale his infinite love and veneration for her. The idea is to put one's hand near this odd-looking piece of mummy, which is on the case near the wall and which looks like a piece of wood that white ants have attacked, and to feel a warmth penetrating into one's hand from the mummy and a tingling up one's fingers and arm, whilst making a wish all the while. The old man told me, much to Mona's amusement, that I was 'angelic', by which we gather he meant 'spiritual', as he told me repeatedly that I was a very strong medium and it was a very rare gift. I have been told this before at spiritualist meetings but have never felt disposed to do anything about it … I'd much rather not.

Mona is allowed to stay on nights until I come off on the 12th so we are going to Cairo. She has also been able to bring about an outing for us and a dinner invitation, from a Mr and Mrs Ades, Jews, whose son is a volunteer in the army and is a patient in one of her wards. It seems they are wealthy people and it will be interesting to see inside one of their homes, which look most sumptuous from without, at least.

The ward is fairly quiet tonight at least, except for coughs and such like. Athenordon, the Greek, is better it seems and Rifleman Smith, our special bugbear, has had his plaster removed and now is on a Balkan beam and has a pin through his ankle. He does seem more cheerful and looks less tired. Poor kid, no wonder he was so miserable with those awful plaster sores. I quite like Smith now. Upstairs in B11 things are more settled too, although Graves, a New Zealander, died there last night. In the PM today they found a lung abscess and TB lesions and amoebic dysentery. The struggle was too much for him, which we could see at first, as he was a pathetic figure, I always felt.

November 30th 1940

Mona and I got up today at 2pm to see the film *Balalaika* which we meant to do yesterday but it was raining at that time and, glad of any excuse not to get up, we decided against. It really was a delightful film, 'The music in my head long after it was heard no more' as the poet sayeth. We were just leaving the mess this morning when the phone rang – after me. It was Frank speaking who said that Bill would be in Alexandria today. So we saw them both in the foyer of the cinema before we went in. Bill looks so tired but she is the same otherwise. She went back by train, leaving at 4pm.

No admissions to B Ground this week and I am glad to say only one or two upstairs. I wrote to Mali and Gwen last night, which I really meant to do a fortnight ago but have slipped badly, I fear so far. Cold today, really cold. I shall have to look out my winter woollies. Odd letters still drifting in from General. This last one addressed to British Medical Service, England! In it he seems to take it for granted that I have been 'through the hell of Dunkirk'! When I think of our pleasant month in La Belle France, of the almost entire peace of it, it makes me smile a little …

The boys are coming back after the concert, making a fearful din, singing and whistling to each other, just as I have got the ward dark and everyone asleep. It would happen. Now everyone is awake again. Smith has been put on the dangerously ill list. Today I was worried about him as his pulse was very unsteady. I can't think why they don't take his leg off and I'm sure it will have to come off in the long run, if he doesn't die first, which he probably will, poor kid.

December 12th 1940

3.45am

I have just come back to B Ground from taking over the report book to CIW for the last time – I hope – for at least six months. Mona and I finish up tomorrow morning but aren't allowed to go away from Alexandria. The big push has begun and it was announced tonight that Sidi Barrani has fallen and that we had taken 4,000 prisoners and some of the wounded, we hear, are expected here early this morning for the huts.[22]

I am very glad indeed to be off night duty. The report last night was painful enough to read but completely agonising to write. I found that in the morning I had written that Athenordon's 'pulse was very thin' yet I had not the slightest remembrance that I had taken his pulse all night, so why I should have elaborated on it is beyond me. I've had the greatest struggle this time to get my 'short and simple annals' written at all. The ward has changed rather in the last fortnight. We had very few in at first but now there are more than 80, many of whom are Australians. Poor Rifleman Smith died – the worst leg I have ever seen. The poor kid must have gone through absolute hell for many weeks. An awful pity they didn't remove his leg weeks ago. Then we had a youth of 20 admitted with multiple shrapnel wounds. He developed gas gangrene and although I rang up the orderly medical officer and they rushed him to theatre at 3.30am, he died before coming back to the ward: a sad business.

Then, there is a case of Mona's: a survivor of the *Warspite*. He came in here with a history of insomnia and night hysteria and as a result of weeks on the *Maine* and incessant air raids, he's had two lots of shrapnel and had been through Narvik as well as Taranto. So no wonder his nerves are frayed. He's been very good really, sleeping quite well but getting fearfully depressed at times. Today he had a cable from the War Office saying that both his parents have been killed in air raids on Liverpool last week. His younger brother and sister had fortunately been evacuated to Canada at the outbreak of hostilities. Poor Morris, no one had been near him all day – I suppose they would feel that he wanted to get away – but he did want to talk about it and go over and over it. I felt that he did so I went to sit on his bed, which I imagine is still *verboten*, and stayed with him for a very long time. Poor kid – he feels that everything beneath him has crumbled away and he hasn't seen any of his people for over the three years and now they won't be there when he does go back.

Then there is Hetherington, an Australian, who has been very ill and Chapman, who is on the DIL and NYD lists. Such nice boys and, of course, there is Stewart, who has been transferred to the huts. He is ready for discharge and goes on Friday so I shall see him again. And now tomorrow, for a sleep! 'Hark, hark, the dogs do bark' everlastingly here and the cats scream and scramble without – a noisy country, Egypt.

December 14th 1940

I have just made myself some coffee on Beatrice at 7.30pm and hope shortly to get to bed for the night. This is the end of our leave and tomorrow Mona goes to AIW Medical, and I to Hut 5, Surgical. Only 56 beds so it won't take long to get to know the patients. I remember how hopeless it seemed when I first went to B, with 108 beds.

Events have been moving fast in Egypt in the last three days. We have taken 40,000 casualties and the RASC has been instructed to get supplies for 60,000 prisoners here and we are told they don't know where to turn to get food. There is no doubt that they will, and have, become a problem for, of course, the poor wretches have to be fed. There is a rumour also that Sollum has also fallen, or soon will. That leaves Egypt practically free but I suppose we shall continue to push on into Libya. It looks as if Mussolini's number is up, as there is also talk of revolts in parts of Italy.

There has been a marvellous moon for nights and we haven't had a plane over. Quite a change. They had one convoy in at 1.30am, but although everyone was on call, it wasn't necessary to get everyone up. It seems, however, that they are expecting a large convoy in tonight and everyone is on call again. Those who successfully escaped and are in town have to ring the mess every two hours. I was to have gone out myself with an

MO from the 11th General but he didn't turn up; presumably, he couldn't get away either. Mona, however, is having a first fling and has gone out with Hugh Bebb to a cinema, unless she is recalled to Monseigneurs later.

We've had a very delightful leave and actually, we are better off financially at least, not having gone to Cairo. We slept most of Thursday, got up and had some tea and went into Alexandria by train and managed to do a little shopping before going to the pictures. It was the *The Light that Failed* (from a story by Kipling) and a more depressing picture I have not seen for years. At the interval, Mona spotted Bebb and said there was someone with him. After the show they beckoned to us and we met them outside. The other one turned out to be Major Jones and it was decided to go to the Carleton for dinner. It was quite bright there if rather too bristling with uniforms. We danced and ate alternately which was very jolly. The cabaret was only fair but we enjoyed ourselves. About 11.30 we decided to move on and try somewhere else so we ended up at Monseigneurs, which is more continental and less military-naval and we liked it better. We did some more dancing there and left sometime after 1am. It was heavenly driving along the Corniche home again with a full moon glinting on the surf with golden light. Lovely.

We had arranged to meet next afternoon, all four of us, and go walking for a change. In the morning Mona and I dashed out for more shopping and had coffee and a ham sandwich at Harricha and then out to the flats again, in time to meet the men at the station at 2.30. It was a beautiful afternoon, very warm with brilliant sunshine; so odd for winter time. We were about 20 minutes in the train, I suppose, and got out at El Marama or some such village, having passed en route the King's Palace and little else but squalid villages, and sand and palm trees and then still more sand and more palm trees. We started walking along the road with the usual string of small boys following us, very black and filthy and charmingly attired in the oddest mixture of clothes imaginable. One had a bright pink skull cap which he obviously cherished. A muddy stream ran along the road side, and it seems this serves the villagers for drinking and washing purposes.

People seem happy enough, however, sitting about in the sunshine, idling, presumably without any responsibilities. We saw a number of water wheels along the banks of the stream, worked by a donkey. They were blindfolded, with straw casings over their eyes, and walked endlessly around and around.

We came at length to a path and left the road for sand and still more sand. The only vegetation was sand, trees and a few odd plots of beans and potatoes, usually hedged around with rushes or pampas grass. We were walking towards the sea and very lovely it was when it came into view across the sand hills, deep blue and very calm. There was nothing to spoil the scene at all and nothing indeed at all but fishing boats and the men casting their nets as they have done, I suppose, for hundreds of years. Aboukir, as it came into view, looked like a coloured picture in an illustrated Bible. These places have changed so little in the years between. We had tea in the local 'pub' – on the terrace, as the winter sun went down, orange, over the desert.

We left by train about 5.30pm and got back to the flats about 6 o'clock. Mona and I changed into mufti, which, of course, is strictly *verboten* and Bill called for us at 6.45 when we met Jones and Copack, ate at the Metropole and then we all went on to the pictures. I was awfully sleepy and remember very little of it. Afterwards we went on to Monseigneurs for dinner and danced for a while. We had to be back at the flats by 11.30 however as a convoy was expected at any time. Today I slept until nearly midday whilst Mona rushed into town to the little Romanian dressmaker who alters and stitches for us these days and when she returned I had lunch ready on the balcony where it was lovely in the warm sun.

Well it's over now and tomorrow we start work again. I received some delightful snaps of my nephew Bruce last night and he thinks of me, Glyn says, as 'a fine fellow on a camel'. He wants me to send him one and so I shall, bless him. I had quite made up my mind to send him a wooden one that I recently saw in a fascinating shop, the Sherif Pascha. It is 50 piastres but a lovely piece of work and I'd love to send it to the child. I believe they will send such things directly from the shop and that makes things easier for me. I must get something really nice for each of the others too as soon as I can manage it. But now I must fill my last water bag and crawl into bed and I fervently hope that I am not dragged out of it before morning.

December 19th 1940

I went to Hut 5, Minor Surgical and Polish wounded, which is lit only until 5pm. After that I was told to go to Hut 4 – eye cases – admitted the previous evening – 65 of them. The place was pandemonium when I arrived, with a fearful mixture of unshaven men, kits, sand, dressing things and nursing staff falling over each other in an effort to restore order. I've been there since, although it's not final even now I fancy, and I like it very much. Thorn, who is in charge, is elderly but a great sport, never interferes or dodders, and works like a Trojan. Bennett, who has just come with the rest of her CCS to help us out, is also with us: an awfully nice girl and long may she stay.

The orderlies are nothing short of stupid and incompetent and the sick berth attendants are not much better. I've quite made up my mind that very few men are any good at nursing, even of the most elementary variety. There is some sort of order established now and quite a number of patients are up and about and they help in the galley and round and about. They are a jolly crew generally speaking and I believe that they are much happier with us than if they were back in the desert. I expect it surprises them that they are being treated like ordinary human beings – indeed the attention, the food and the clothes are exactly the same as our own men receive. We are having the greatest fun picking up a few words of Italian. Those that we do know we work overtime, but they enjoy our efforts and we don't mind at all.

Bill is up in Alexandria on leave. They have been hectically busy in Helmieh, getting a lot of casualties that we missed through not having any room. Among the boys whom we knew on the ship is the one who has had his foot blown off, an Alun Griffiths, who is seriously ill from some war injury. He was from Harlech and such a nice lad and I do hope he'll be alright. Bill doesn't look at all well and I do hope she will pick up with these 14 days' leave. She hopes to finish up at Luxor.

I arranged to purchase another iron on my last half-day off. I wanted a French one similar to the one we got at Cairo, whilst they are still available. The struggle I had was unbelievable. I had priced one a few weeks ago and they told me 125pt. I was horrified and after telling them that I had got the same thing in Cairo for 80pt, I departed in high dudgeon. This time I tried a bigger shop, and they had the effrontery to ask for over 200pt for the same thing exactly. I told them exactly what I thought about it, and of them, and bounced out. A few shops further down they asked me 150pt and, although that was better, I said I'd wait and see. Nothing happened so I marched off back to the original place and this time they asked me to pay 140pt. I looked very grieved and told them that only three weeks ago they had told me 125pt. They agreed but said that everything had gone up twice since then. After a long discussion, he completely floored me by asking how much I would like to pay. I could not think of any answer to this one, so we agreed by closing the deal at 130pt! Really, these Egyptians are the limit. They think that because we are British we have plenty of money and they put their prices up as soon as they see us entering the shop; it really is too bad. I'm going to be more painstaking in future – it seems to pay – at least I hope it does.

1941

Alexandria – Cairo – Ismailia – Hospital Ship *Karapara*
Suez – Aden – Bombay – Basrah

January 31st 1941

I've allowed this to lapse for about six weeks, which is sheer laziness and now I shall have forgotten so many things that have happened. I see I was in Hut 4 when I last wrote herein, but we closed down the day before Christmas. I went to AIW Medical for a few days then but as soon as the next British convoy arrived, I was packed off to Hut 1. Miss Thoms was in charge and we got on very well together, although she was a bit of a muddler. I was very happy there when Matron suddenly decided to send Mona and me on leave.

Continued February 21st

We didn't want to go because (a) we hadn't enough money and (b) with only a few days notice, and 14 days required, we couldn't go to Palestine. This broke our hearts entirely but Matron seemed to think it was now or never and so we decided to go anyway. We thought we'd have a few days in Cairo en route and then spend the bulk of time in Ismailia. There seemed to be nowhere else to go in Egypt, except Luxor, which didn't quite fit our bank accounts at the time. We booked our seats on the plane to Cairo but the day turned out to be so filthy – a terrific sand storm – that the plane didn't go and we had to go up by train. We got talking to a charming Egyptian – Sabri Batos – who was in the Ministry of Agriculture and he asked us to go to tea at his sister's house the next day. We went and found them a delightful family, the sister, three small girls, a boy of 18 or so, who was a medical student at Cairo University, and a friend who was a doctor. They were all Coptics as distinct from Moslems. We were given, or I should say 'forced into', the most exotic and enormous tea that we have ever seen, and then we went again to lunch the next day and to the zoo and the Gardens of Mair afterwards.

We spent these two nights at Shepherds where lying in bed and ringing for breakfast gave us the unbound satisfaction that it is possible only for two weary nurses to know! We arrived at Ismailia about 10.30pm and taxied out to the United Services Club. The room we were conducted to almost made us weep, enamel beds and red blankets! Busman's holiday! The club however was superbly situated on the shores of Lake Timsah through which runs the Suez Canal. Sitting on the veranda in the warm sunshine, it was heavenly to look across the lake at the far shore, with honey coloured sand hills and groups of dark palms, and away to the right the high road that runs on its desert way to Suez and Port Said. The sweet water canal that runs through Ismailia was always crammed with barges and ancient wooden craft that looked as if they'd been in the same spot since Cleopatra was a girl. Their tall curved masts against the sky were strangely beautiful.

The town itself was hopeless: dirty and uninviting, but the French gardens were very lovely indeed. We stayed two nights at the YMCA and the rest at the club. We drove out to the Australian hospital one afternoon. Enid Baker had come into town in the morning on a day off and it was marvellous to see her again after many days – and then once again I met Jean Oddie. She is just the same Jean and I felt mean to let her slide out of my days for so long a time. We had tea in the mess, a long narrow brick hut, and inspected the tents and huts in which they lived. They seem happy enough there; their uniforms are very nice indeed and much superior and more sensible than ours are. Jean came into the club on her day off which was the day before we left and we talked and talked. While we were going over the old days, by coincidence, an airmail letter came for me from Connie Short, which mentioned Jean.

We left next day for Cairo, travelling up with some RAF men we had previously met and who were bound for the Sudan. We had tea with them at Grappi's before seeing them off on their long journey to the desert. We stayed the remainder of the time at the Metropolitan Hotel which we liked very much. Our old friend Bimbashi Abbas Ali came up to meet us that night and he and Mrs Jaques Bewish took us to dinner at the James, and then to the film of *Rebecca* afterwards which we'd seen in London, so found it a bit boring.

Next day Bill came out, having a day off, and we all went to the tattoo given by the police at their barracks in Abbasia. It was a grand afternoon, sitting there in the glorious sunshine, watching the superb Arab horses and their riders, balloon shooting, tent pegging and Cossack riding. We went to the Bardia, a night club, later to see some Egyptian dancing and then had supper and went to bed. We also met, through Bimbashi in Cairo, a charming couple, Mr Baileu, who was

Swiss, and his wife, a Jewess. And two very gallant gentlemen, Felix and Ralph Green – also Jews and very wealthy bankers. Felix lives in Alexandria and Ralph in Cairo. Ralph asked us to go and see him next morning before leaving and we did. He has the most amazing collection of treasures I've ever seen. There was much too much to take in at one glance; odds and ends from all corners of the Orient, Greece, Japan, China and Palestine. Dear old Bimbashi came along to the train to see us off and bought us a box of sweets each; he really is the kindest soul I have ever known and he just can't help it.

On return from leave, I was sent to A2 W (Dysentery) with Miss Silb in charge. They were very slack and Silb is delightful to work with but I was there only three days when Matron sent me off to Hut 9. They were frantically busy there with a new convoy of badly wounded men, mostly Australians. I hated it at first but got to like it very much, as usual, so much so that about a week ago I was really disgusted and disappointed when Matron sent word that I was to go at once and open Hut V for Italian Medical. I've never been in charge before and my head spun round counting sheets and going over the equipment with Steele from whom I was taking over.

We started out with about nine patients for B1 but odd ones drifted in and then the next day we got a convoy of about 16 patients and we really had a busy time for a few days, until most of them were evacuated on a convoy a few days ago. Keary is with me at the moment and three orderlies who come and go in addition to five Italian orderlies who remain. Surgeon Lieut. Phillips is the medical officer and quite nice to work for. It's quite a picnic getting anyone to understand what I want to know and what I want them to do; but somehow or other under some special providence for POWs, they have all so far survived. Today we have been made all medical, so perhaps it'll be more straightforward from now on.

Duncan rang me on Tuesday. I hadn't heard from him for quite three months and I had thought he might be in Greece or even killed. But it seems he has been in the desert, Bardia, Tobruk and the rest, and is back in his original camp for a while. I went out with him last night after 8, which is, of course, strictly taboo. We had dinner at Le Petit Coin au France and then drove home and talked for a long time. He looks graver and older but is not so very much changed, although he thinks he is. It is nice to see him again. I had a letter from Major Dalt too, from the Abyssinian border, I imagine, at the 11th IGH and from Ted, who was in the Bardia, Tobruk and Dernia[23] business and who is now convalescing in Palestine after some slight illness. Padre Helman has also arrived in Alexandria but I've seen him once only as they left to go up to Tobruk some weeks ago but were turned back before they arrived and are back now at the King of Maru hotel again. Mona and Hugh and Major Jones and I went to the Union club on Saturday night and another night Mona and Hugh and a Polish officer and I went to the pictures and to dinner afterwards. Oh and I went with Cpt. Marshall to dinner at the Carleton one night. That, I fancy, is the extent of my gallivanting since my last leave.

But Mona and I had a delightful day off on Wednesday. We caught the bus out to Aboukir about 1 o'clock and lay on the sands under the palm trees. We wore mufti and took our lunch with us and I wrote to the family. It was heavenly to get right away from the army atmosphere for a few rich hours. In a letter from Mother this week, I learn that Clwyd, 'little Clwyd', has been appointed to Port Moresby, Papua New Guinea. How we Parrys are getting around the earth! Poor Mother: how she will hate the thought of it as it will mean two years at least, I suppose. I hope he doesn't get malaria or any of those horrid infectious diseases. I can imagine Clwyd in a topee and shorts – very dashing.

I'm glad I've written this up to date. I'm on a 5–8 shift and have suddenly had the urge, as well as the time, to do something about it and I mustn't leave it so long again. Japan is becoming very disagreeable and would like to stir things up in the Pacific. Well, who can tell which way the wind blows?

March 31st 1941

It's exactly a month since I wrote this up – very disgusting really as so much and so little too has happened. The Western Desert affair is drawing to its logical conclusion or so we are led to believe. Gerabub and Keren have fallen at long last and most of the crowds who were at Benghazi and round about are now waiting to set sail for Greece, Salonika or some such spot. Turkey is still lying doggo but German troops have taken over Bulgaria, which made no resistance at all and issued an ultimatum to Yugoslavia, whose government signed a pact within its axis, but who, a day or two afterwards, overthrew the government, the regent and his wife fleeing the country and the young king taking over. So good for Yugoslavia and its people and its eighteen-year-old king. Yesterday, we had splendid news of the fleet in the eastern Mediterranean, three cruisers and two destroyers sunk and no loss at all to our ships or personnel. We were told to stand by last night for seven officers – but none has so far arrived – and it transpires that only five casualties came to us, to B Ground as usual. It was a grand show – good old NAVY. The officers were thrilled and as excited as boys, even the commanders!

I am in Officers now, where I went about ten days ago and like it quite well. We aren't busy and Mona is in charge, having taken over from Kirsten, who is on sick leave. I have sixteen rooms to do, comprising mostly senior officers, naval and military, majors and commanders and what nots and two head cases, one a young RAF fleet officer (of Duncan's squadron), a nice lad, and another fractured base of skull, a Norwegian from a minesweeper who was beaten up in the town last night. There is a nice Australian lieutenant commander who, in a taxi accident, unfortunately lost the sight of one eye, and then there are one or two other Victorians on the ward.

Duncan came back out of the blue, or out of the desert, about three weeks ago but has been transferred recently to Cairo to do ground work duties for three months. I rather think he has become somewhat unnerved after the desert business anyway and he doesn't trust himself flying at the moment. He brought us some yards of the Italian parachute material, pure silk, white, a lovely quality and I shall get it made up into blouses or something. Ted came back for a night last week too, from Mersa Matruh. He has been back with the regiment beyond Benghazi but they are just waiting now to go off to Greece – probably gone by now, I think. He is completely fed up with the army and utterly disillusioned with the war in general. The usual thing, I fear.

The padre came down to the ward recently and has been up at Gerabub and was very thrilled about it. He said it fell in two hours at the last stages. He brought me a piece of broken pottery and a little saucer as souvenirs. Mona and I have gone all Australian in the last week or two, with the MO, Colonel G., field ambulance and a Captain Mac. We and two other Melbourne MOs with Annie Nixon and Teddy Head had a jolly party at the Hussein Club on Saturday night and we fell into bed at 3am. I am really dead today as a result.

The weather is warming up nicely at long last. It has been so cold and soon I know it'll be too hot. We go into whites soon – a doubtful advantage. Anyway it'll be something to get out of black stockings.

Enid Baker and Jean Oddie have had leave and have each spent three days in Alexandria. It was delightful to see them.

They came out here and had tea with us on our balcony and later we took them over to the hospital.

April 5th 1941

Benghazi evacuated by us. Not so good.

April 6th 1941

Germany declares war on Greece and Yugoslavia and hostilities begin. Addis Ababa entered by British troops.

April 8th 1941

Massawa[24] taken.

April 9th 1941

We have evacuated all Western Desert towns officially as far as Tobruk, but rumour has it as far as Mersa Matruh. This is a great shock to Mona and me and, having just had our supper of tomato sandwich and coffee, we are finding ourselves in a state of stupor at this last bad news. It all seems so incredible and swift. Well, the next move that we must consider is possible evacuation of the hospital. I hope this isn't defeatist but it is quite on the cards. We can't decide what to take and what to leave, but we have definitely agreed to leave our tricolenes and black stockings and to take my *Albatross Anthology* in case they don't go in for poetry in German concentration camps!

The wireless news tonight reported that 2,000 of our men have been taken prisoner and three of our generals are missing, probably captured – Cannon, Gambier-Parry and Tree. I had a letter from Ted yesterday telling me that instead of being sent to Greece he is being sent to the OTC but I fancy his course will now be interrupted. Actually, although we are talking extravagantly and laughing and saying '*malesh*'[25] in the best Egyptian manner, we are very worried at this news. The Greeks are cut off in Salonika also.

April 10th 1941 Good Friday

Mona and I went to a non-conformist service in the hospital chapel. Two very nice young padres took the service but only about 12 of us there.

April 13th 1941 Easter Sunday

Mona, Bill and I go to church again.

April 14th 1941

The blow has fallen! I am being transferred to a hospital ship. I feel absolutely dead when I think of it and all that it entails. Seven months here in Alexandria with good friends everywhere and now to be thrust solitarily into the mess of a hospital ship – how I shall loathe it. If only Mona and I had been sent together, it could have been different, but now – well goodness knows – if ever during the war, we shall see each other again. *C'est la guerre*. I don't know the name of the ship yet or where she goes and where from, but now I must get to work and pack and how!

April 16th 1941

I haven't gone yet. Still hanging around in a state of chaos and confusion. This room is a depressing sight but I feel too weak to do anything about it until I hear more definitely what I am to be doing. I had a half-day off today and don't need to go on until 1pm tomorrow. So time for a sleep in. I forgot to mention that the *Velta* was machine gunned off Tobruk and sunk. Blunden was on her, but everyone was saved and the staff are in our mess, having lost everything. A cheerful prospect for me.

April 30th 1941

And still here. Although Matron tells me that I am still on call, I doubt very much whether I shall be transferred to a hospital ship but I still live in and out of my trunk, which is somewhat trying.

We've been evacuating Greece for the past week and part of their army has capitulated. I suppose the poor things are weary after all the fighting in the past six months and one can't presume to criticise them, although we are told that the 5th column is rife there, as it has been in all countries that have fallen to the Nazis and we have been betrayed over and over again. The Australian and New Zealand troops seem to have been pushed to the fore again, and as before, have given good account of themselves. It remains to be seen if they will all get out alive as the Germans have been in Athens for some days and I suppose will do their utmost to cut them off. One can't help thinking of the troops all the time and of the families who are wondering where they are and what is happening to them.

We ourselves are more or less CB at present. Only a special military pass will get us into Alexandria and even then we have to be out of it by 7.00pm. No one knows quite why this is but there are rumours of riots and impending air raids and troop landings and enormous convoys preparing for Greece. The latter is the most likely, I imagine. Mr Churchill has spoken and even he doesn't sound over-optimistic for the moment. I can't help thinking we will be evacuating Egypt before too long. I hope I am wrong but I can't see anything else for it. And then where? At the moment we are holding the Germans in the Western Desert, though they are beyond Sollum, a few miles inside the Egyptian border. The Tobruk siege is holding out, we are told, and Dessie has fallen to us which should free many of our troops there. John has been in hospital with phlebitis on his elbow but is now out again and presumably back with his regiment. Luckland, who was to have been married about a fortnight ago, has heard nothing from her fiancé until a few days ago. She was terribly worried as he is in Tobruk and can't get away. I've had letters from Colonel Green and the padre, both it seems in the Western Desert. I don't know whether Ted has rejoined his regiment or is still at the OTC, the latter I hope. Otherwise he will be caught up in Greece, as his regiment is there – the 21st.

General's son Bill came up to see me yesterday and, although I had half a day and was in the flats, no one had enough sense to tell him so and I missed him. I fancy he was on his way back to Palestine, or else back to the desert. PO Strong is back from Tel Akabir and on a fortnight's leave. He came up to the mess the night before last, somewhat inebriated, I am told, and demanded to see 'old Parry' and couldn't be got out! I was in bed blissfully unaware of what was happening until Mona told me he was at the flat door. She advised me not to go down to him and lectured him for a good half hour. I promised to have dinner with him last night at the Beau Rivage if he hadn't drunk anything all day. He didn't, so we had dinner and I lectured him again for his own good. But I feel awfully sorry for these boys, particularly when they are on leave. There is nothing for them to do in this place but drink, if they don't know anyone to talk to. It is all very sad but they look so pathetic and lonely and they are missing so much because of this war. Sometimes I think to myself I shan't do anything about it, I simply won't go out with them and then, I remember that tomorrow, next week maybe, they may be dead. And I change my mind. Mona thinks I am soft, but I'd have more to reproach myself with if I refuse them an hour or two occasionally. After all, we haven't given up much in this war and it's little enough to do for our fellow creatures. I know I am right in this, although it mightn't always be wise. But, 'It is not wisdom to be only wise and on the inward vision close the eyes. But it is wisdom to believe the heart'.[26]

May 1st 1941

One hundred and sixty sisters arrived at Fairhaven for lunch – back from Greece. Mostly they are from New South Wales, Queensland and Tasmania but I am told there are none from Victoria. They escaped with a hand case and what they stood up in. They say they have been machine gunned and dive-bombed all the way and had to leave their stretcher cases behind, but the Greek doctors promised to look after them. An awful thing to have to do – I dread the thought of anything like that.

Last night Cecil Duncan (RAF Ismailia) came up and collected Mona and took her off to dinner and the cinema. He had another RAF lad with him and I was asked to go too but was, fortunately, on duty. I have promised to make up a foursome on Friday night – but I really don't want to go – can't be bothered being polite and sociable to stray pilots who come up for a few days. Still, 'malesh'. Eric Darwoon has been very badly smashed up it seems and was on the DIL but is now getting better. I must write to him if I can find out what hospital he is in.

We have a Yugoslav general in Hut 10 W. He is Chief-in-Charge of the Air Force and has compound fractures of his tibia and fractures of both radiuses. Dozens of gilt-braided Ruritanian-looking gentlemen come to see him by day and by night. His aide de camp is in the same room and his doctor is always within call. It is all highly diverting and everyone is in a pronounced FLAP about it, or was: the colonel and DDMS and, of course, Matron. He badly wants to be fed by one of the sisters but the colonel has decided that one of the orderlies must feed the gentleman. He has already told me that I am like the Yugoslav women, who are very 'beoooootiful', and asked the doctor to tell me that if he were a captain or a younger man he would … The rest was somewhat obscure and certainly purposely mistranslated by the doctor. All very interesting if embarrassing. The aide de camp had pentothal this morning to have his shoulder pain reduced and, on coming round, suggested that I should sit on his bed and hold his hand and what he told the doctor to tell me still remains unknown – fortunately, I think. But that too was interesting, I feel. They don't waste time on formalities, these Yugoslavian gentlemen.

We heard today that a destroyer with a complement of 1,000 crew and troops coming back from Greece was sunk and only four men were rescued. Seven ships with 1,000 troops on board at least, have also been sunk. But the papers report that we have only 3,000 casualties against 60,000 German ones so it could be worse, of course. There is a convoy of wounded coming in now. A lovely warm afternoon and everything looks entirely peaceful but one wonders for how long.

May 7th 1941

Night duty

This came as a complete shock, Matron sending us amok the previous evening. We knew it was coming soon, but I fondly imagined I would escape, as I am still supposed to be on call for my ship. Mona is in A Ground and I am in Hut 7 – Officers' Medical. We are full and even had to open Hut 8 for two naval men off a convoy from Tobruk last night. I have an excellent orderly with me for a change, a Yorkshire boy, really reliable and sound, which is more than a comfort. I asked him his name the first night and he said Ealey. I thought it sounded a bit odd, but imagined that he ought to know and thereafter called him Ealey in good faith. I found later from someone else that his name is Healey, so now I pronounce the H, but still feel he likes the other way the best. Selk is night superintendent and who could be better? Bedwell is on and Mullins, a very amusing Yorkshire girl whom I like more and more, and Rippling, a recent naval acquisition. The rest are fairly colourless at the moment.

May 13th 1941

Night off

I am sitting at 7 o'clock of a cool and pleasant evening, on my balcony, with all night in bed before me, breakfast in bed in the morn, as I wish, and a new and just possibly a comfortable pair of shoes to put on when I go on duty again tomorrow night. What more can a girl want after all? I feel so much at peace with the entire world that I could almost write a sonnet. I would call it, let's see ... *On first sighting a pair of white, probably comfortable shoes*. It would be good if I had enough energy to woo the muse – alas, dead these many days. For if ever a poet felt strongly about her subject this one would be hers. It would come straight from the heart, and deftly handled, it would be enough to make even the strong weep ...

The seas still roll in, waters from the entire world, in endless motion. Ships on the skyline, merchantmen and fishing boats with sails of pure poetry. Ali leans over the balcony near me and insists on gabbling to me in Arabic of which I understand three words, '*suchac, quais, mucquais*', from which I gather – rather brilliantly, I modestly think, that the heat was bad but the heat is now '*mafish*' and the night cool, which is good. Ali is right and Ali is a poet, a philosopher in his own land. The donkey carts go by, bells all a-jingle, the peasant vendor ambles serenely along, and the last rays of the sun catch the glass jar on his capable head. Now he is one with yesterday's 7,000 years. There are some sailor boys in white shorts and jackets pedalling past on bicycles; now an air force AC with his Greek girl, now a Tommy with his girl. Now an ambulance, now a despatch rider in a hurry, now a taxi with a QA correctly attired in her beautiful tricolene and with a suitable escort. Now three Egyptians, complete with tarbushes, in a sidecar and a family going home from the beach in an opulent limousine. Now some transport driven by b-topee'd Tommies *avec* tin hats. The door banging below is one of the safragi admitting one of the girls coming off duty … endless activity, and as varied and colourful as life itself.

I am enjoying my ward – I'm not busy at all, although there is always a mad scramble to get beds made o'morning. I have Hut 8 Isolation to supervise as well where there are only two, both convalescent, nice boys. One is writing a book and hopes to publish it in America – I hope he does. As one has chicken pox and the other scarlet fever, they can't foregather so each sits on his little garden wall in the cool or heat of the evenings and converses with the other across the ten yards of sand. So, one feels, governments should sit, in the cool of the day unhurried and in philosophic mood, with ten yards of this good earth between them and a kindly word of 'good-night' before turning in over their respective garden walls. But men are stupid in the mass – and never will learn. Individually, I love them all, at least at some times and in some moods.

The men in Hut 8 greet me affectionately I always feel, although I don't see much of them. Curtis, RAMS, watches over or so I hope. Just now by night – Hut 7 is my spiritual home – the men are mostly navy these days as the RAF and army are evacuated very often to other parts, just as they are nicely settled in. They are mostly young or youngish and a nicer collection of men you couldn't wish to have. I like the ward to myself at night and I feel they are all happy to be there, which is a good feeling. There are some things which are more satisfying to me than medals and good reports and being popular with Matron and having the equipment correct or having the ward perfect on the colonel's round. Little things that I can't write down here or tell anyone about, because they would seem unimportant and in a sense conceited – although of course that doesn't come into it at all – things that the men say to me from time to time, when I do simple little things for them to make them comfortable, real gratitude often clumsily expressed – golden words that send me on winged feet on my way and give me satisfaction in this ghastly business. There was a Danish captain on the DIL – he was moved to the Anglo-Swiss because our place was too noisy in the daytime and there wasn't a room to give him – who patted me on the hand before he went and said with a sweet sad smile, 'Your name should be Miss Nightingale'. He's probably dead now. And a midshipman who sent me a note on the back of a section of the daily orders early this morning – presumably because he didn't like to tell me himself – 'Sister, you were awfully sweet to me, early this morning. Thanks a lot.' This because I merely went and stayed with him for a minute or two during the air raid. I know how they unnerve him; he was on the *Southampton* when she went down and then on the *Huntley* when she went down.

There are so many things I should like to have remembered, but they don't really matter, only the remembrance that at some times one has helped. These are the things that no one can ever talk about, the trivial things, which surprisingly enough become permanent and add considerable sweetness to the days. If by some chance I should become a war victim too, and who can tell who may or may not be – I should hate to think my name was inscribed on a brass roll of honour – as though I were some heroine – which emphatically I am not, and should be perfectly happy knowing I had done my job according to my own standards – although they may be a little odd at times.

We had lunch with three Australians today, nice men: one from Queensland, one from Sydney and one from Donald in Victoria. They drove us back to the flats. They are flying to Cairo today and return here tomorrow – then back to Mersa Matruh and the dust and the sand storms. How they remain so cheerful these days, I can't think.

May 22nd 1941

HMHS Karapara[27]

The second phase has begun.

When we were dressing to go on duty last Monday, a note was sent up to Mona and me telling us to pack at once and be ready to leave forthwith on a hospital ship. We dashed up to the mess and were told that we would be required to go on duty until midnight. The ship was HMHS *Karapara* and Miss Scot-White was to be the theatre sister. The rest of the staff were being transferred except for the Indian girls who were in our mess pro tem. We felt rather numb about it all, especially Mona, I expect, as she didn't even know that she was destined to come along too. I was distinctly annoyed, for various reasons which I shan't be able to remember when I read this after many days so they'd be better left unmentioned. I hated the thought of leaving the men in Hut 7: Westacolt, Symmers, Stewart, Arnold, Haynes, Sarnham, Rigby, Hogg, Lautar, Browne, Downing, Sang and the rest. And in Hut 8 Piggott, Hooper, Johnstone, Davies and so on. In Isolation are Cornish and Cope and, more recently, my old friend General Merkovitch and his *Capitaine*. Sad indeed.

And the men were so sweet about it. I felt they really were sorry that I was going. I never felt a happier atmosphere in any ward I've worked in, no one could have been nicer to me – I loved them all. I left at midnight after having made a round of unofficial farewells. We had supper then and walked down the road in the Egyptian night, to the flats – for the last time for goodness knows how long. I wrote one or two letters and then went to bed, too weak to attempt any packing until morning. Then I was up fairly early trying to restore some order among many hundreds of trunks and cases and we had coffee on Mona's bed, Beatrice being in commission for the last time. I left her behind *avec* saucepan. Then some of the night staff came up to say *au revoir*, including Teddy, Bedwell and Jockey, and we left by taxi for town about 10.30am, visiting Khan Khibil for some money and doing some last-minute shopping. A taxi back to the flats and then we went up to Fairhaven for lunch or rather in order to see as many girls as possible who would be there for first and second lunches at that time.

I'd only been there about three minutes when I was told that Rochester wanted to speak to me on the phone. She asked me to go over to the ward for a few minutes as the men had something to give me and wanted to say goodbye. I was quite shaken about it as, of course, one never dreams of farewell presentations, on leaving a ward in wartime. But I had to go, very hot and bothered, and feeling totally undeserving and extremely minute. Pigalt was on his break when I arrived and they gave me the packet, which I opened. I was never so surprised in all my life to find a travelling clock of brown leather with my initials on the front of it: luminous, alarmed and eight day. A perfectly lovely clock – something I never dreamed I should possess. I could have wept, not so much for the gift itself and its worth, but for the thought that had produced it. Pigalt told me that he had gone round first with the thought of a modest box of chocolates, but they gave so liberally and willingly it grew to this. He was so sweet and told me in all sincerity, 'You have no idea the esteem in which you have been held, Sister'. So I went around again, in my *boootiful* tricolene, blushing furiously and shaking hands and muttering some sort of thanks to all and sundry.

This is something that goes much deeper than having a mere present given to me. I know now, and I knew before that really, I had the real affection of every single man in those wards, although I was there only two weeks and could do very little for them at night time. And I knew, alas, that I'd rather have had just that than any RRC or OBE or empty glories of that nature. Well – it's all behind me now with promises to look them up if ever we are anywhere near HMS *Ajax*, *Formidable*, and *East* ... and all the rest, and promises to write. We probably shan't – still it's nice to feel that way about it at the time. We hated leaving Teddy, Bill and Lynnette and oh so many others we've been with for so long but thus it was and so at 3pm we scurried off for the taxi to catch the train at 3.45.

It was a long tiring last journey to Port Said. Miss Baldwin was with us – the ex-matron of this ship – and Hood, a New Zealand girl, who had only been on her for two months and was now posted to Helmieh and had to go back to the Ralapala to recall her baggage. We didn't arrive in Port Said until 1.20am and then we were taken to the Eastern Exchange for the night. Next morning up betimes we presented ourselves to the RTO at 9am and then to the ship by launch. There she was well at the mouth of the canal, white and green with large red crosses on her – our future home for the ensuing six months, I suppose. We were taken to meet the CO and then on a tour of inspection around the wards and theatres. Quite nice really.

We have our own sitting room and the officers can come over the threshold if asked! We will dine together but at our own tables. The IMS girls join the ship tomorrow probably. We are waiting here patiently until we can get through the canal, until it is demined and the ships preceding us have gone their ways. It seems that six have moved through today, which means we may go through with the next batch unless Jerry decides to come and lay some more mines tonight. It is the sort of game that he plays – as soon as the coast is clear or almost clear and the ship all ready to move off, over he comes again to hold up the works. It appears that we may take 200 or more convalescent patients at Suez; anyway we are bound for Bombay where on arrival we shall lie in the dock for perhaps two months, for repairs to damage done in Tobruk this last trip. The ship was dive-bombed and had direct hits and has large holes through several decks and shrapnel holes through many of its walls. They had 500 patients on board, all of whom have had a really frightful time but got back to Alexandria on one engine, which will take us, we hope, to Bombay.

Mona, Scotty and I have quite nice cabins and there is an iron and ironing board and altogether we are extremely comfortable. Everyone has been most kind and helpful and I feel we shall be very happy here if the monsoons don't lay us too low. The commanding officer and second-in-command, Major Duncan, are British IMS but the rest of the medical personnel are entirely Indian – Hindus and very charming men. The crew and all the orderlies are Indian, with the exception of two British orderlies, and the officers and the captain are British. Whilst in port we have to go to bed by candlelight and, of course, we are completely blacked out, so hurry on 'orders' so that we can sail all in a glitter of lights. What a day, or night rather, that will be! So now we have to think in rupees and annas, heaven preserve us, and it's only a few months since we got used to piastres and milliemes.

Germany has been landing troops in Crete by parachutes from gliders, over 3,000 of them. Most of them, it seems, are out of action for some reason or another, but Churchill doesn't belittle the business at all and says we must hold on to it at all costs. Perhaps they'll turn us round and sail us for Crete. Who knows? How we shall miss letters – beyond everything.

Matron, Miss Tyndall, came up on deck about 11pm and seems very nice [...]²⁸ She is Irish and has an excellent sense of humour, which will help considerably. We went ashore in the afternoon and had lunch at the Casino place opposite.

May 23rd 1941

The IMS girl plus Wright and Goodrich came aboard last night. And here we are at 3pm sailing up the canal, having left about 10.30pm and lying up for an hour further back. We shall probably tie up near Lake Timsah, Ismailia. Shades of our last leave. We actually saw the ship that we are now on at anchor when we were there and we even met Matron – Miss Baldwin – in a shop there. And we had our grey blouses on, which she said she admired very much!

It's getting hotter. We have to have a typhoid inoculation tonight as it's rather overdue.

May 24th 1941

Anchored in the Bitter Lake last night and we had to get up for an hour and a half for an air raid warning. We were very annoyed having our sleep disturbed last night and today is very hot. We passed Khartoum yesterday and I had hoped I'd see Jean or Enid among the bevy of beauties bathing on the beach. But didn't. I gave them all a wave however, for the sake of old times. Yesterday, also, I was dressing for dinner when I heard from some desolate spot on the shore as we went by, 'Spot any Aussies on board?' I nearly leant out of the porthole and shouted 'yes' but hadn't the energy. Such a barren and parched-looking shore on either side with outposts the whole length of the canal to watch for the parachutes that tell where the mines fall. The canal is 87 miles from Suez to Port Said and we have 27 miles to finish, today, I suppose.

May 27th 1941

Anchored in Suez now because we didn't get away on Sunday as we had thought. After bringing the pilot on board and taking him off half a dozen times, we actually got underway. There were two danger zones where we went dead slow so as not to disturb the acoustic mines which it was thought were dropped here during the air raid two nights ago. I certainly heard a plane go over the ship that night. Once onto the canal we were safe enough and it was an amazing sight to see the wreckage of odd ships sticking out of the water. No wonder there is a muddle with the shipping: one unlocated mine in the canal holds up all the ships and some-times for weeks. No-one could have any idea about such things unless they had actually been through and seen it for themselves.

We got into Suez the night before last, ships of all sizes and nationalities in the bay around us, including two destroyers and four other hospital ships – *Manunda* (Australian), *Tyreah* (British), *Manganni* (New Zealand) and the *Llandovery Castle* (British). We didn't go ashore until this morning. Mona and I went across in the launch to Port Tewfik, ostensibly to see if we could get on board the *Manunda*, only to learn that she had sailed for Australia early that morning. So we went walk-ing through the tree-lined street of the little port, a perfect day with flame trees and oleanders and frangipani. While I was admiring the flame tree, an Egyptian passing by came over and, grinning, said, 'You like it Missus?' And thereupon snapped a small bunch off and presented it to me and went on his cheerful way. It wasn't his tree, of course. They are awful rogues these Egyptians but likeable often times.

We took on coal at Suez. It was a fantastic scene to watch in the evening light. The great barge, flat and still and low in the water, the natives seemed more incredibly filthy than anything one has ever imagined, clad in the most amazing collection of rags possible, each with a gleaming silver identity disc on his wrist, gifts of a grateful coaling company I suppose! Raking the coal into large raffia baskets on the floor of the barge, they hoisted them onto their heads and walked up a long standing plank to the barge's side, then along the narrow ledge, their feet pattering over the sharp fallen coal and along another plank which led onto the ship's hold, then down again to begin all over again.

It reminded me of something I can't quite remember, a frieze, an old painting, a scene from an opera, even a ballet: the little ragged filthy procession, pattering endlessly up and down. It had a certain artistic effect, the odd colouring among the rags they wore, the quiet sky, the green oily sea and the great ships lying around at anchor. Not to mention the incessant chatter and screaming and arguing that went on among them every single moment of the many hours they were there.

May 28th 1941

Off again at 6am, bound as far as we know for Aden, but no patients thus far at least. Getting awfully bored.

The news is rather depressing this morning, except that the *Bismarck* has suffered the fate that she dealt out to HMS *Hood*. The Germans appear to be establishing a foothold in Crete although we are, it seems, sending reinforcements. The New Zealanders appear to be doing some counter-attacking but with what success it is difficult to ascertain yet. The king of Greece has escaped to Egypt. The Germans have forced us back a short distance at Sollum also. I hate the thought of moving away from it all with nothing to worry about: safe with every comfort. How I loathe it all … I never wanted to come on to a hospital ship and certainly not this one. Besides, it is very difficult indeed with prevailing attitudes to the Indian personnel. Well I suppose it will have to be endured for six months at least.

July 4th 1941

Bombay

More than a month has passed since I wrote herein. Now the first fine careless rapture – if there ever was one – has passed long since, and I expect lots of things have happened that I shall forget to record.

To return … we reached Aden on June 2nd: Aden with its grim barren cliffs and the sun pouring down relentlessly. We went ashore in a launch in the morning and I nearly passed out with the heat. We were told it was 125 degrees the previous day and it couldn't have been much less that day. I bought some cotton material and made it into a frock on returning to the ship. Mona and I went ashore again in the evening with Bruce and Major Ramchandani to the open-air cinema. It was rather lovely sitting there with the starry black night above us and all around, high above the walls, the fascinating corrugated peaks of the mountains. The picture was an old one with Jack Colbert and pleasantly silly.

We left next day and about midday had some mild excitement when a native craft hailed us and asked for water. There were about 40 Somalis who had lost their direction and had run out of water. It pleased me to think we could stop and help them, it was so hot to be in an open boat and to be without water would be dreadful. It appears that ships are not really allowed to stop in war time but I liked our captain the more for doing so. After all we were a hospital ship and should be above rules of that sort.

Next day we ran into the monsoon and from then on until we put into Bombay, there was no peace or comfort anywhere. I wasn't seasick at all but the dining room didn't see me for quite four days. The smell of cooked food and the sight of the knives and forks chasing each other across the table were too much for me and I knew it. The old ship creaked and groaned, lurched and tossed and rolled – in short, did everything possible except sail completely upside down. At night, in bed, one was either standing on one's feet or alternatively on one's head. Distinctly unpleasant. Then on deck, one struggled out and flopped into a chair and stayed there until it was absolutely necessary for some particular reason to get out of it. We were completely fed up with it after a week. The news at this time was depressing too. Crete has been evacuated and at what a price. As usual no protection for the troops from the air. I am told the Welch regiment was there among others and goodness knows how many Australians that one might possibly have known. It doesn't bear thinking about. A bad raid on Alexandria also makes me think about Bill and the rest of my friends.

We reached Bombay on June 9th and that evening went ashore with Bruce and Frank to a cinema and Chinese restaurant for dinner. Next morning, *avec* luggage, we left the ship and got ourselves established in the Majestic Hotel, where I am now writing this. We would have preferred the Taj but, '*malesh*'! This isn't so bad except that the one and only lounge is very public and everyone drifts in – for all the world it would seem – for drinks, any time between now and midnight. Mona and I, as usual, have a room together, a large one, with a little writing room annex and a bathroom, which is a great comfort to us. The weather for the first fortnight was hot and rainless, and then the monsoon broke and the rains began. It comes down in sheets, and then suddenly clears, but it never gets cooler, only stickier and hotter and steamier than ever. We go to the cinema quite often and usually on Friday or Saturday and, if asked, to the Taj for dinner and a dance afterwards. We went to the Kanday beach on one occasion for a swim and we've been for the odd drive and a cocktail party at Major Ramchandani's.

The market claims a good deal of our attention and we get odd frocks made as we live in mufti here. We live on advance pay from the paymaster but have managed to get the remainder of our accounts transferred from Barclays at Alexandria and that helps us through. We have spent lots of money as we always do in a new country and with nothing special to do with our time, it is always fatal! Bombay is a fine spacious city, with wide clean streets and lots of trees and some noble buildings. I am interested in the Congress men who wear white hats. I always feel they have the utmost contempt for us, when they pass us by. And well they might. I respect them for it, because I feel deeply sympathetic about their grievances, which are very real. Good luck to them: they'll have home rule in India before many years are out and I hope they make a better job of it for their people, especially the poor of the land, than we have ever done. It shouldn't be too difficult.

Russia is in the war now. How crazy it all is. Things don't seem to be going too well for her either, from today's news. America is helping us as well as she can with supplies of all kinds and I expect she'll come into it completely when she is ready. We have got back Damascus and Palmyra from the French (Vichy) and there have been very few raids over Britain for many weeks, for which thanks be!

Only three letters since we arrived and those addressed directly to the ship and sent by air. One from Hooper and Johnstone (shades of Hut 7) and one this week from Bill Williams who is sorry we went our ways so soon after meeting again in Alexandria. I wish I could hear from home as it's about eight weeks since I heard from Mother. I sent a small book to Bruce today – he'll be grown up before I see the lad. Too bad.

We are all getting fed up with each other. Scotty is remote and too intent on a social life. Wright gets strange passions on any writer she may be reading. First it was Jane Austen, and then it was Katherine Mansfield, then Gertrude Bell. She talks on and on endlessly and no one gets a chance to say a word. Anyway it's not without effort of trying because she only cuts across you before you've finished and you trail off weakly and wonder why you began. Mona has inspired lifelong devotion in the breast of the conductor of the hotel orchestra, who asked her to marry him the second time he saw her. He is an Austrian and bangs around looking soulful and miserable by turns, because she had to decline, with thanks.[29] I, it seems, quite unbeknown to me, have inspired a similar feeling in a man called Potts who wears glasses and who comes morning and evening, sitting solitarily at a table, somewhere in the lounge. One glimpse of the glasses and I pass by, aloofly, like Beatrice. All very romantique. So do we waste our days.

We are supposed to sail about the 15th of the month – but time will tell. Matron is still away on leave, and Goodridge, I am sorry to say, isn't rejoining the ship but is being stationed somewhere in India. 11pm now so I must get to bed … to sleep, if I can, i.e. if I don't lie awake scratching as I've done the last few nights. I've had awful bites on my legs from some mysterious creatures I've never seen – bugs, sand flies or ants. If I have any trouble tonight, I'm going to get into the bath and stay there until morning.

July 5th 1941

Another night of scratching. I didn't get up for breakfast, being too exhausted after thrashing about all night. It was a really bright moment, however, when Mona brought in an airmail letter from home, which included one from Dad also. My sister Mona, it appears, is on the brink of being called up.

July 21st 1941

HMHS Karapara

We came aboard again on Saturday, 7.30pm. Yesterday we spent the entire morning packing and unpacking and I took a short – or rather I should say prolonged – course of 'death' as Miss Tyndall calls it, until it was time to get up and go to dinner. We played over our newly acquired records on deck before retiring for the night, then bed, but I don't seem to be sleeping at all well. Perhaps the bed is too narrow or it might be the ants – I had an enormous bite from one on my right shoulder blade the night before – quite three inches across and red and swollen. And such a minute ant too!

But these are minor events compared to all that has happened during our last week in Bombay. Momentous happenings and decisions in a very few days … and without tempting fate too far in these precarious days, I can at last record herein that I have become engaged to one Kenneth Hannan Stanley. This was decided upon on the 14th July, but we decided to break the news to Mona and Harry Wright the next day.

We had a somewhat hilarious party at the Taj Harbour bar on the Wednesday night and went on to Green's for dinner afterwards and danced a little before Ken and I left to spend the rest of the time left to us together. Next morning we had breakfast together and I went down with Ken to the docks to see him safely installed. I didn't want to see the ship depart – neither of us could have faced that – and so I went back in a taxi in a complete daze and Mona and I went out and drank iced coffee – I think – and did some last-minute shopping, including at the market, where I bought some materials to keep me occupied on the ship and which, with any luck, will form the nucleus of my trousseau.

Ken's ship was very small and looked extremely uncomfortable, especially for negotiating monsoons, so I expect the poor darling will be feeling rather unhappy for various reasons. They thought they were calling at Aden and then making for Port Sudan. Now we hear that we too are calling in at Aden and it's just possible, if they stay there a day or so, and they do fewer knots than we do, or hope to do, that we may contact them again. But that seems much too good even to imagine so I am not allowing myself to think about it. (Of course, I could write volumes about 'us' and all we mean to do *après la guerre* but this isn't the place). We are at anchor now, some distance from the shore but we can still see the gateway and the Taj. We expect to leave this afternoon and I shall be glad to get away in the circumstances but shall always welcome the sight of Bombay in the future as all our letters will be collecting there. Our mail did arrive about three days before we left. I had more than 25 letters and magazines from Mali: letters from nearly everyone – several from Mother, Glyn, Clwyd, Gwen, Mali, Gwerfyl, my Ruthin cousins, General, Leo (who sadly is in a sanatorium), Bob (presumably in Tobruk), Arthur Green living in a cave, PO Strong from Alexandria and Deaney and many others. What a lot of good friends I have in so many corners of the earth and how much richer life is as a consequence.

Russia seems to be holding out very well, and we appear to be doing things in France and Germany through the RAF. Otherwise there seems to be a lull in the Middle East.

August 6th 1941

We arrived in Aden on July 27th – a Sunday and Mona's birthday. Fortunately, the monsoon treated us very well on this trip apart from some pitching, which didn't affect us at all, although most of the staff, including Mona, seemed somewhat upset. She and I were sitting on the portside of the ship in the afternoon and a ship passed us quite closely. It seemed to me that it looked like the *Rahmani* but I decided that it wasn't as it looked rather larger than she appeared to be in the docks. She went by, and a few minutes later, when she was still in sight, but too far to do anything about it, one of the officers informed us that that it *was Rahmani*. I felt so mad to think that I had been unaware of it, as she passed, particularly as Bruce, who had been on the bridge, told me that he had seen someone waving frantically on deck.

I feel sure Ken would have known he was passing the *Karapara* as we were the only hospital ship there that day. It seemed incredible that we had only anchored here about an hour and that the wretched ship should decide to go away, just at that time. Well of course even if we'd both been using glasses and had seen each other we could have done no more than wave across the intervening stretch of water – I know that. But to think that we had been so near, and that I didn't realise it, was what hurt me so much. I knew only too well that he was going off into the unknown and it might be months before we should meet again. Oh well … I watched the ship with glasses until it became merely a smudge on the horizon and then with a wisp of smoke it was gone.

We are still sitting on the same spot of sea, having been in once to coal, but neither Mona nor I went ashore. I have been doing some sewing and reading but generally speaking it is hot and breezeless, especially today. Ships from all over the world come and go, as noiselessly as the smoke that escapes from their funnels – British, Norwegian, Swedish, American, Dutch, Egyptian, Greek, Free French, Belgian and many more. They lie around for perhaps an hour or two, or perhaps days, and then next morning when we get up, they are gone and only the wind knows where. There have been many cruisers in and out as well including HMAS *Australia*, and an aircraft carrier which we heard was the *Formidable*, well known to us in our Alexandria days. I've just counted more than twenty ships on our starboard side and, by raising my head, I can see quite twenty five or thirty to port.

The new Dutch hospital ship which has been handed over to the Australian and New Zealand governments, an enormous ship with lovely modern lines which makes us look thoroughly insignificant in comparison, has been and gone. The South African ship *Arva* came and went too, presumably both to Suez, and today the *Aba* came in.

This seems, with Bombay, to be our spiritual home. Actually, we are hanging around here until the *Vita* arrives, which should be in about five days' time – or so we hope. We have heard that there is some mail on shore and as soon as they can get the launch across, it is ours. But there has been a swell on these last two days and so far we wait and not without impatience. There is a cocktail party tonight to celebrate the first anniversary of the sailing of the ship as a hospital ship. Instead of dinner, a cold supper will be served at 9pm, which is more sensible. And thus we serve, who only stand and wait. The war drags slowly on. German troops are still trying to get into Leningrad but so far the Russians seem to be putting up a good effort and have escaped heavy casualties. Libya is quiet but Alexandria and the coast as far as Suez have had bad raids these last moon-lit nights. On the wireless last night it was announced that 70 people had been killed and 150 wounded. So I suppose we ought to be glad we aren't sitting around in Suez, but such is human nature, we aren't a bit pleased at our good fortune.

August 11th 1941

Heading for Bombay once again! Quite suddenly on Friday evening (8th) word came that we were to sail for Bombay. The captain, 3rd officer, two engineers, Major Ramchandani and various others had gone ashore to get the mail, after breakfast. They made one attempt to get back by midday, but it was too rough to get the launch alongside so they returned to shore. It wasn't until just before 7.30pm that they were able to come on board (the swell was still bad) and then the captain was told by the first mate that the orders had come. We weren't told when we were to sail so Mona and I feverishly wrote to John and Ken, thinking this might be a chance of getting them away before we left Aden. But alas for our zeal for when we awakened next morning, we were well out at sea and Aden far behind us. We are also led to believe that our course has been changed and that we are now to be taken over by the Indian army. There is great speculation as to what will become of us. It certainly appears on the surface that we shall come this way no more. Half of us think it will be the Far East run, Penang or Singapore. Well, well, whatever next, I wonder. I don't think anything will surprise us ever again. So near Australia and yet so far.

Well, Mona and I have mixed feelings about this change. Mona hasn't actually seen John for ten months and she had reason to believe that he was somewhere within reach if we had continued our usual course. She was itching to get to Suez and then of course all this. I don't know what I want at all until I know where Ken is. There is just the merest chance of course, even if there is a lot of wishful thinking about it, that being in the Indian army, he may be sent out to the Far East also. The Sudan is finished and it is just possible that they will send out some seasoned campaigners to this new front, where trouble seems undoubtedly to be brewing. I hope so much that we won't be sitting off Bombay,

Madras or Colombo for months on end just waiting for patients. We have done so much of this – it's just on three months and not one patient so far – it is so absurd. Well anyway it's not our choice and we can't help it, although it is poor consolation for the lack of something definite and useful to do.

So now we are ploughing through the Indian Ocean once again – Bombay bound. We have caught the monsoon again this time and last night and today have been every bit as bad as the first trip out. I'm writing this on deck, starboard, my feet on the rails, a woolly frock on because it is inclined to be cold and a scarf tied refugee fashion, according to Mona, around my head. The wireless is pouring forth weird strains supposed to be bagpipes I think (terrible), whilst the ship rolls up and down like a drunkard after a particularly successful 'beat up'. Now I know what is meant by the mountains and valleys of the sea. Except that it is a bit awkward trying to walk about and that it's next to impossible trying to eat gracefully at the table. One is awakened many times in the night with the sounds of shattering glass and tumbling furniture, and most often one tries to sleep on one's head or, alternatively, on one's feet instead of in the usual horizontal manner. It's not so bad really, at best it's cool and there is a fresh wind blowing. It was the heat that laid me low the first trip when I couldn't even think of the dining room then, but I eat my omelette o'mornings these days, monsoon or no monsoon. This omelette tradition does not go back very far, it is true – only to the last fortnight or so in Bombay. I never remember eating a cooked breakfast heretofore but it occurred to me that I ought to eat an egg a day – as I rarely touch meat – and that the only time one had an opportunity was at breakfast. Thus it began and somehow an omelette doesn't look quite as wicked as a fried or poached egg, first thing in the morning. I can't guarantee that this is to be an abiding institution and I don't know that I feel any more energetic for all my extra protein absorbed thereby.

I have been reading quite a lot. Lady Fortescue's *There's Rosemary – There's Rue* was very delightful and most interesting and *The Humming Bird* by Eleanor Farjeon a most enchanting delicate fantasy. Lady Eleanor Smith's *Lover's Meeting* gives an exciting uncanny feeling that perhaps there is something in witchcraft after all. Refreshing in these days. Now I am reading *Take Courage*,[30] a chronicle of the Civil War in England which ends rather beautifully. Peninnah remembers:

> And this I say: Take courage. I have known trials so bitter that my whole course seems darkened. But I have known joys too: putting one with another I have found life too good to miss; I am glad to have been born. Again, I have lived in times so troubled that I can't think this nation has ever seen the like, or will ever see the like again. But the land has not perished; the sun shines, the rain falls, the sheep still feed on the Pennine hills; women still conceive and bring forth and give their children suck; and while man lives, the hope of righteousness will not die. The strife is sore while it lasts; yes it is very sharp and bitter and wearying to the spirit, for it seems as if it will never come to an end; but if we keep a good heart and cease not to care for justice and truth someday the storm will pass and the nations rejoice in the sweet air of peace.

That was over 300 years ago and we seem further away than ever from the 'sweet air of peace'. Does it matter so little to man then – the grief, the bitterness and the loneliness of the 'years that take the best away', that he strives so little and so half- heartedly for peace. This is the second 'great war' in our short lives and this one involves us all in our generation, how much we do not yet know. My sister Mona is waiting to be called up. Glyn in his last letter tells me he is going to ask the bank to release him. His doctor is not quite satisfied with his throat at the moment but will examine him again in September. He has talked it over with Edna and apparently she agrees with his going if he feels he must. It is sad for her and little Bruce but there it is. And my Ken too. Well it doesn't bear too much thinking about; in fact it hardly bears any thinking about at all. I shall write some letters.

August 28th 1941

Ken's birthday!

On the move again – this is the third day. We left on Tuesday at 4pm, sealed orders coming aboard the previous afternoon. It isn't Madras and the Far East – yet anyway. Things have begun to flare up in Iran. She was rather too kindly disposed towards Hitler's minions, so our government after at first being polite, then firm, took things into their own hands and walked in. Russia obligingly walked in from the north. They are meeting with some resistance and have even encountered German and Italian soldiers, although it seems rather vague, just at the moment.[31] So we are bound for the Persian Gulf, for a change, Basrah, as far as we know.

The monsoon hasn't entirely spent itself and the new IMS sister is still prostrate and some of the others look rather green, but I've been grand and mean to keep so. I think I can say with some truth that I'm a fairly good sailor now. Soon we are told the seas will grow calm and the heat will begin. It is the height of the summer in Iran and Iraq just now so it promises to be jolly. As long as we have nothing to do we may just survive. It's beautifully cool now, a fresh breeze blowing. I am writing this on deck, starboard, the sea pleasantly ruffled with white horses and bottle green between. Some sailors in their navy suits and colourful scarlet sashes and caps are doing something with ropes for'ard. Major Ramchandani, Mr McDonald and Mr Singh (the Sikh with glasses, such a nice fellow) and Mona are playing darts with as much interest and concentration as I hope our statesmen may manage in winning this war. Mary is knitting assiduously, behind me, a jumper in pink wool.

I think we are always glad to be on the move, although on the homeward trip we can never move quickly enough because of the letters that may await us. I did very well last time. Twelve came abroad from the Ballarat estate from various people including the padre, Tad and the colonel. The padre is still in Tobruk and dismal food and inferior water are, he says, taking their toll, although he is fairly fit himself. I am quite sure he is a great help to his men and he does love them with all their frailties. Tad is still, as he says, 'in the process of becoming a gentleman!' How he does love the irony of all this snobbishness. The colonel seems well, if a trifle bored. He is in charge of the occasional clearance of wounded from a 'certain important centre' – Tobruk, no doubt – and in-between-time they live a modified caveman existence.

We were sent ashore next morning and to the Taj for two nights because of some readjustments to the ship. It is so much pleasanter there than the Majestic but I believe I have got a soft spot for it, even so. Well, I ought to because it was more than kind to me although it's probably unaware of that! Of course we would strike a Bank Holiday that first day, which meant no money or letters. We all had about two rupees each but somehow or other we managed to get to see *Gone with the Wind* that first night. The colouring I thought was superb but I don't like Clark Gable, although I suppose his acting was good. I thoroughly approve of Vivienne Leigh but I thought the whole film was rather long and certainly too intense in these war-riddled days, anyway. And normally, tragedy appeals to me so much more, so I suppose I am too near the real thing nowadays. Next morning, up betimes and straight away to Lloyds for letters of course. I kept saying to myself, 'There probably won't be any from Ken,' so I wouldn't be too disappointed if there were not. But to my intense delight there were five letters and two long ones from Mother. Great excitement. I read and re-read Ken's all afternoon and wrote to him care of the Kemprenal Camp in Cairo, his temporary address. He was so sad about our ship being so near in Aden and that he could attract no one's attention. Alas, so was I.

I've had two letters since, one just before we left Bombay this time and one the previous day. The last one gives me his permanent address, 5th Indian Troop Transport Corps MEF. And it sounds as if he may be at Amerya near Alexandria for he asks me if I want him to get in touch with any of my friends. He also mentions that he will be contacting John in the next few days as he has had none of my letters, which is rather disappointing. I particularly want him to get the first one I wrote or else it will be difficult for him to pick up the threads, as it were. Perhaps it may arrive eventually. I have sent him a small present for his birthday – nothing much – it is difficult to think of things which are useful and not too bulky to carry around. Moreover, on my not very magnificent salary I can't afford to buy the things I would really like to give him. But he won't mind that. I managed to get a cable away to him for his birthday, the morning we left. Bruce took it ashore with him – he has now left and has been transferred to the *Sudara* and may be going to Australia so I do hope he gets it today. It may cheer him up a little, particularly if my letters haven't yet arrived. And I would like him to know that I am thinking of him today. He little thinks or knows that I am heading for the Persian Gulf at this very moment.

I've had letters from Mother, Father, Glyn and Edna, full of good wishes on my engagement. I must have told them all that was required for Mother seemed quite stumped for questions, which is rare enough. No doubt she'll think up some for next time. They all seem genuinely delighted and thrilled and I felt pleased that they felt so happy about the whole affair. Roll on the day when Ken and I will arrive home *après la guerre*. What a day that will be!

September 6th 1941

Basrah in mid-stream – Shatt-al-Arab

We arrived at the mouth of the river at dawn on September 1st. Gradually as we went slowly up stream, the scenery became more interesting, the river banks lined, as far as the eye can see with date palms. Odd picturesque craft appeared – balhams with lovely lines, like Flecker's 'olden ships'[32] and white butterfly sails flitting among the palms along the canals that opened up every hundred yards or so along the river's bank. Collections of mud flat-roofed huts, two somewhat dilapidated grandiose harems belonging to some late Shah, an odd incongruous-looking modern bungalow, then suddenly tall black chimneys against the sky and we were passing Abadan, a large oil refining town with great oil tanks and a highly industrial air. We actually arrived in Ashar about 1pm and the anchor went down. We are in mid-stream and no distance from shore. It is a fine clean broad stream and one of the pleasantest places possible to be anchored.

Basrah itself is about two miles or so inland. As towns go, Ashar is quite unremarkable – one or two possible buildings: the best, the Port of Authority Office, which has a dome and pillars and is, I suppose, 'easternly modern'. In Basrah itself there is a mosque with rather a good mosaic dome and muezzin tower – quite modern, I should imagine. The town itself is dreary; a narrow canal runs the whole length of it and the buildings on the one side, sheer with the canal bank, and the graceful curved balhams gliding up and down the canal give the place a faintly Venetian air, at night anyway, with the moonlight lending a certain beauty to what in the glaring light of day must, I fear, look dusty, mean and drear.

The first night we were there Mary went ashore with a naval lieutenant who had come aboard from the naval authorities and who, I imagine, wanted some company for the evening. She came back with an invitation for Mona, me and herself to go for lunch next day with the captain of the *Islami*, a British ship we had seen in Bombay. It was frightfully hot going out at midday and we didn't exactly relish the thought of it. The naval launch called for us and we started on the long delightful trip up stream to Magil, about four miles away. We met the captain, a nice man by the name of Kerr, Major Cash, Indian Army (how glad I am that Ken does not resemble this type), Danny, the little lieutenant who had taken Mary out the first night, a Lieutenant Commander Hardwicke, who is in charge of the docks here and not long out from Scotland. We had lunch on deck, quite a jolly party, including a lot of nonsense pertaining to the chicken in the curry. Then we retired to the captain's sitting room and played darts. This occupied us until teatime and when we were about to leave, it was decided that we would all go to dinner that night. So that meant going back to the ship to have a bath and change and then another trip back to the ship. By that time the party had increased by two, a regular QA who ropes us in for such things when the occasion demands, and a certain Mr Hibbard who possessed among other talents the gift of tongues. We went out to the Dir Pal Hotel and had dinner and danced quite a lot on the improvised floor on the lawn. It was pleasant in the garden with the music in the air, the coloured lights, the swing, garden seats and full yellow moon.

Mr Hibbard called for the three of us next morning about 9 o'clock and took us in his car out to Zubair. We passed through Basrah first, along the canal skirted with the eternal date palms, gum trees and hibiscus. Most of the buildings are made of soft yellow brick; some parts of them are very old and dilapidated, but as the old buildings crumble and decay, and new ones replace them each year, so they hope to widen the street and improve things generally. All the women seem to be wearing black. On the outskirts we passed the jail, the hospital and the cemetery, all rather comfortably adjacent. Then the desert – the last dusty barren waste of desert, with miserable tufts of grass and occasional salt bushes. Of course, there was the mirage so tantalising and maddening to be lost in the desert. We passed the tall broken column which is called Sinbad Star from which Sinbad the sailor is supposed to have started out on his travels. Odd groups of horsemen passed us with their curious headgear and their panniered Arab horses.

Then there was the extraordinary spectacle of about six or seven dromedaries laden with palm leaves which, as the beasts ambled along, waved and gyrated against the sky like some weird primitive dance from the South Seas. The bells jingled charmingly as the animals rolled along.

Zubair itself is a complete mud town: a market square, a mosque, Arab horsemen riding in from the desert, black-veiled women; the only modern thing at all, it seemed, was a telegraph system. Gertrude Bell was billeted in the Post Office here at one stage on a mud floor with her own camp bed and so on. Mr Hibbard knew her in the days that she came and went hereabouts. He said she was a veritable terror and everyone was scared to death of her. He told us too that she divulged some secrets later in her life and committed suicide. We didn't know this – I suppose it's true as Hibbard has been here more than 20 years and is a man of some authority. Away to our right were Coab and beyond Mecca and Jeddah. Not far away is Shiba (Beersheba), scene of the famous battle. And

Hibbard told us an interesting story about how we won this important battle. The Turks, it seems, had the upper hand and our CO, who was almost desperate, had the brilliant idea of sending word to Zubair and insisting on every man, woman and vehicle being turned out to join the rest of the army. It had the desired effect: their numbers to the Turks looked like enormous fresh replacements – the illusion was helped by the mirage, which magnified their numbers and the Turks fled. The Turkish commander, learning of the ruse which lost him the battle, later took his life. Near Zubair, too, is a stretch of some miles of crumbling mounds composed of minute pieces of brick – this is the site of an ancient city: 'nothing beside remains – the lone and level sands stretch far away'.[33]

We returned through Basrah and bought some jars and pottery and saw the rows and rows of pots lying like old Omar must have seen them many a time of old. We've been out each evening since, to dinner and once to an open air cinema and, always the most delicious bit, where we step into a balham at the wharf and, with two stout oarsmen, are punted safely home to our ship. Thus it ends. We have gone upstream this morning to Magil and are now alongside our ship. The patients are supposed to be coming on about 5pm. We had hoped to go out tonight but I'm afraid we shan't although Bob is up with the Captain now, trying to work the oracle. We shan't be allowed, I'm sure.

Later

We weren't allowed but we went all the same. To the airport first and then we went and sat in Hibbard's garden in the moonlight where we emptied his refrigerator and ate cold chops and Welsh rarebit at 2am. A memorable occasion because *verboten*! 'Ah, moon of my delight.'[34]

September 28th 1941

We arrived back in Bombay on September 12th after an uneventful trip. We had only 21 patients in C Ward, and only two of these were in bed and not ill at all. It was unbearably hot in the Persian Gulf and, down on the ward 'with the potatoes', it was perfectly dreadful. However, our orderlies are so good and there was so little to do in any case that we didn't have to do anything other than put in an appearance now and again. The one piece of excitement was when Major Ramchandani restored the speech to a boy who had been completely deaf and dumb through shock. He had been through the Spanish war, Norway, Dunkirk, Libya, Greece and Iraq; he was with the Australian Army and 47 men around him had been killed with one bomb and he alone was left. Also he had lost nine members of his family in England so it was little wonder he was suffering from shock. Major tried various electric rays on him to begin with, and we gave him sterile water daily for about four days (which was purely psychological, of course), then, nothing happening, the medics took him to theatre, put him under an anaesthetic and spoke to him as he was coming out of it, telling him that he had already spoken to them (which he hadn't, of course). The boy insisted that he hadn't, whilst shaking his head – but they said yes, he definitely had, and then he just spoke in complete wonderment and delight. It had been over two months since he had heard or spoken a word. We were all so thrilled and the boys in C Ward quite looked on it as a miracle, and crowded round the lad who, of course could hardly believe it himself and couldn't stop talking.

We saw all the patients ashore next morning, en route for Poona.[35] We had scarcely got to know them and it seemed a pity to see them go so soon. There was a young red-headed second lieutenant, not my patient, who had tried to commit suicide three times before coming on the ship. I had a most interesting chat with him on deck. It was awful to know that he was under strict guard day and night – always an orderly with him – enough to send anyone 'mental' and he was most sensitive about it. We had a strange conversation about modern poetry, pacifism (he was a pacifist) and nationalism – he was a Scottish Nationalist – and we talked about India. According to all the laws of the Medes[36] and the Persians we could both have been shot for sheer heresy. As it was, he was considered mad and so put under guard while I was still at large, but no one knows for how long! It's a queer world. This boy Dunnett was the son of a well-known Scots Presbyterian minister from Edinburgh. I feel so sorry for the lad.

We went ashore then and to the bank but no money had been paid into our accounts (nor has it been now on the 28th of the month) so I drew out my last 15 rupees, leaving about Rs2, I fancy, and thus equipped, we installed ourselves in the Grand for the weekend. We visited the paymaster on the Monday and after a lot of cogitating he decided he would pay us, there being some recent amendment to his list, in which he feared at first that we were not included. It was a slight relief, naturally, as we were on the brink of poverty.

We went to the church on Sunday and to a party on the cruiser *Hector* on the Monday evening. Mona and I were roped in to have dinner with the captain and his guest, who was a commander of a Greek destroyer, and so we spent the evening aboard. The captain had superb quarters on the old Alfred Holt ship. There was a lot of head-turning about our staying to dinner and it was all rather amusing, although annoying. Anyway, they could have stayed instead of us for all the good it would have done them, as it happened. We went aboard next morning in a tropical downpour and put out into mid-stream where we still remain. The *Atlantis* has been in for maintenance but she left yesterday for England, home and beauty, we believe. The *Talunda* is still here although rumour – which is rife – has it that she leaves any day. We stay on board most days, sewing, reading or writing. My correspondence is such that I could and should be writing all day long and every day.

The day we got back to Bombay I received 22 letters, several packets of papers and an anthology of verse from Mali, dear Mali, how thoughtful and generous she is. I had two letters from Ken in my bundle informing me that they would not be long in the Middle East and might be crossing the canal. The next one proclaimed they were in Iraq and still the poor darling had not had a single letter from me. I felt so sorry and wrote at once to the new address and cabled to say I had written frequently. Since then I've had two more letters, in the first of which he acknowledges two letters and my first cable and in the second, two more letters – earlier ones certainly, but at least as he says, letters. I feel so pleased about it. It seems that having spent 12 days en route through Palestine and Transjordan they have arrived back in Iraq, where they are now about to 'unfold their tents like the Arabs and as silently creep away'[37] again, back whence they came, or so they think. It all seems rather mad, but Iran is now quite quiet, the king has just gone off to Argentine or somewhere especially remote and his son is on the throne. Now, with Russia still fighting grimly for Leningrad and having re-occupied a number of villages out of Smolensk, the position in the south is rather precarious with the Kief gone. It is expected that there will be a big clash in the Crimea with, on one side, Turkey and, on the other, Bulgaria forced into it against Russia. So one day, or another, we shall slip out of Bombay to some place not so quiet, I suppose.

Yesterday, we left on the early launch and went to church. Then we went on to a cricket match at Colaba, between

HMHS *Karapara* and the Welch! It was pleasant under the trees and watching the match took me back years to cricket matches in Shelford afternoons, when we were young. The Welch won, out of hand, and we all had tea together in their mess. They were a nice lot of boys, mostly from South Wales, I learned. They told me that of the 900 1st Welch that were at Alexandria and who went onto Crete, only 200 remained. They fought the rearguard action there and most of the 900 who didn't get away were killed. It made me so sad to think about it. I received a letter today from Gwen, who is nursing in Llandudno, because her husband Ronald is in Barmouth. The airmail is taking about six weeks to arrive now, a little better. I wish I could afford to send all my letters by air but I just cannot. I've begun to send off Christmas cards and small gifts to one or another. I just can't forget, even in the war, how good they were all to me in those happy years in *Cymru fy*.

October 20th 1941

Still sitting in the same spot of water and no sign of moving yet. I have done nothing of any note – been to the Taj about twice and once went across to Elephanta Island. That was a pleasant day to walk under the shady trees and to see the sea rolling in surf hundreds of feet below us. We had an excellent lunch with a better view and explored the ancient Hindu caves afterwards. It was all exceedingly interesting. Much of the stone work is in an excellent state of preservation and the figures are finely proportioned and executed. It took two and a half hours to get there and the same to get back.

We have had some difficulty about pay again, pending some decisions as to where we actually belong. Nothing was paid in at all for two whole months. I shall not record our actual words on the subject. However, they have deigned to pay us the August salary and some arrears of pay recently, but September's has still to come to light. It appears we are now to be paid from Poona, so this ought to be more definite than the ME, although we are still not on Indian rates of pay. What has infuriated us however is that they have taken out, for the third time no less, an advance of £5 which I drew in France in May last year. Investigations are being made, I hope. They certainly are not getting away with this latest piece of infamy – not if I can do anything about it.

Ken has left Iraq and I last heard when he was somewhere en route to the ME again. It sounded like Galilee or Tiberias as he was going to gather some tiny shells for a necklace for me. He sent me a charming silver bracelet from Iraq for which the customs made me pay Rs10. I feel this was grossly unfair and they were exceedingly nice and they said they would refund all but Rs2.8 of it. So I am more than happy about it. Poor Ken, I don't know whether he realises it but I feel he is going farther and farther away from me. We shall probably never go to the ME again, whilst he is almost certain to be sent to Libya or north, if Germany heads that way. Goodness knows where and how and when it will all end. Japan is threatening again now that Russia is losing ground – Odessa is gone and Moscow seems sorely hemmed in. They have even mined the Great Barrier Reef and Thursday Island. I think we have been at anchor here for quite six weeks this time. I suppose one day we'll be sheared out, if we haven't got stuck to the floor with the barnacles before then. Poor Russia, how she has taken the hurt! Well, I hope we won't forget it, when the time comes for the reckoning up of such things.

Clwyd is in Papua now. Sister Mona seems very happy in her camp hospital. Glyn's throat is still bothering him a lot it seems and Mother's dermatitis seems to be getting worse instead of better. I do wish she would go into hospital so that they could keep a constant watch on her. I have just had a birthday letter from General enclosing a canteen order for ten shillings. Of course,

I can't use it – at least I wasn't able to in Egypt. I'll enquire when I next go ashore. Sweet of him to think about it, however.

We have had two sports meetings with the *Talamba*, our sister ship. I didn't go over there but had to put in an appearance here at the return match. Mary didn't however, and that caused a mild sensation in various quarters. Now they've invited us to tea on Thursday and to stay to supper and a dance later. No one wanted to go but Matron thought two should go and it was decided to draw lots and Marcia and I turned up. We would! I loathe these polite social affairs. It is Diwali, the Hindu festival, this week so shops and banks are closed for at least two days and Tich is running around presenting us all with dreadful sweets, such as they are in India on these occasions, it seems. We tell him they are delicious so he is quite satisfied and then we get rid of them via the porthole. I have had several *John O'London's* and about six *Horizons*[38] from Mali this week. She is so good and we all enjoy reading them immensely – it is a link for me, with a world I was so fond of and familiar with – we never see this type of magazine from one year's end to another.

The harbour is very busy these days with all kinds of sea-going craft from tiny scarlet yachts with snow-white sails to heavy cruisers. The *Exeter* is in and one or two Greek ships. The *Yara* (HMAS of ancient memory) has been in and gone out and there is an Australian armed merchantman beside the *Windsor Castle*, the *Felix Rousseau*, a large Free French ship, the *Orion* with a piece of her bow in some collision or other, the *Strathallen*, numerous breakers and smaller ships of all nations, mostly Norwegian, Dutch or American and even including Japanese. The little island fort near the 'Gateway' seems to be undergoing reconstruction into something really considerable. The docks are stocked with Bren gun carriers[39] and such things for export to the Middle or Far East. Everywhere is activity, although the army itself appears to function socially more than any other way, at the moment.

November 3rd 1941

It was my birthday on Saturday. Mona arrived with burning incense at 7.30am plus two parcels, one a little Peter Scott copy of *Brent Geese Flying in a Mackerel Sky* – lovely! And a set of most exquisite lace table mats. She is so extravagant, but it is no use telling her. Mary gave me a dear little pocket edition of Thomas à Kempis. During the course of the morning arrived letters from Ken, Mother, Mona, Glyn and Edna, and Bruce. I was so thrilled to think that they all arrived on the very day. And Ken's included a picture of himself – a forerunner of a bigger and better one, apparently. This one however is splendid and I am delighted to have it. Mother, in St Andrew's hospital, east Melbourne, appears to be slightly improved. I hope it is true and lasting. Some delightful stories from Bruce. Mona is happy in her camp hospital and, from an extremely minute snapshot, looks extremely nice in her uniform. Clwyd, it seems, is charmed with Port Moresby, although I haven't heard from him so far since his arrival.

I have sent Ken's Christmas parcel off. Such a to-do, thinking what to buy and then packing it and sewing it all up. Such fun! I do hope he has half as much fun opening it as I had packing it. Mona has sent a parcel to him too. I had a parcel of books from Mali – Geraint Goodwin's *Conversations with George Moore*, and the sixth number of *New Writing*.[40] It's so kind of her to do this, so often. Today from Gwen and Ronald, I received Louis MacNeice's latest collection of poems *Plant and Phantom*. Lovely to have some new poetry and they are so good to think about me all this distance away.

I am knitting a pullover for Ken, in a rather nice cable stitch, simple but effective. He has bought a cine camera and I'm terribly thrilled about it. I've always wanted one – there is nothing to equal it for holding precious moments. Just think that the films that he takes now we can see over and over again, 'When we are old and grey and full of sleep'.[41] Only he can't get film in Egypt, he says. I want to try and smuggle some in to him occasionally in the odd, inoffensive looking parcel. Wicked girl! Tomorrow it seems we are going into dock once more for about a week, which means we go off to a hotel, The Grand, I think. We liked it last time – it's quiet and unpretentious.

November 13th 1941

Well, it wasn't the Grand, it was the Taj again. We were herded together in what they fondly call a 'suite' on the fifth floor: four bedrooms and a bathroom minus doors. All very friendly, but we didn't appreciate it. I do like a room to myself. I prefer even my postage stamp of a cabin on the ship to having to share: 'a poor thing but my own'.

The week we were ashore was notable for nothing except that I spent my whole month's advance from the field cashier and almost all I possessed in the bank and have arrived back almost penniless. However, I've been in this state so often since I joined the army, it doesn't worry me much, although it does irritate me to think that they haven't paid us one anna since August and it's now the middle of November. Of course, I did buy myself a frock which I don't care for much and the shoes (wine court ones, which were made to my measurements) turned out to be complete failures. Much too short and I feel so cross about them. They fit Mona quite well so she is wearing them. It was Mother's birthday yesterday so we drank her health in shandy last night. In her last letter she appeared rather better and was going home, I hope not too soon.

I had a letter from Ken too and two not very clear enlarge-ments of snaps taken en route by his CO. However they are most acceptable. He had posted two photographs a few days before he wrote to me. He wrote on my birthday and he said he was celebrating it by packing up and getting ready for the road. He had got in touch with Mrs John the previous evening and hoped to be able to see Monica Thompson that night. I do hope he did because she could then let me know odd things that Ken could not perhaps write himself. I am sadly afraid that they are bound north and east perhaps to the Caucasus as there is some talk of our joining the Russians there. Ken sounded rather depressed and I am so far away – he says there is no hope of him returning to India for the duration of the war – and I can do nothing to cheer the poor lamb up. It's useless worrying, I know, but I find it impossible to do anything else somehow. I want to get off the ship and unless we are frantically busy by the end of the year, I'm definitely going to ask to be transferred back to the ME. Quite apart from Ken, for I don't really think we shall meet until the war is over, I can't bear the climate in India, or at least in Bombay. I'm always tired and lethargic and the nights are scarcely cooler than the days. There is some talk that we may move up to Karachi to hang around there for a while. British Intelligence seems to think we take up unneces-sary space here. Personally, I think they should put wheels on us and run us into a garage for eleven months out of every twelve. That should cover all the work we have to do. Karachi, they say, is much cooler, but then what about our mail? That's the only thing I object to moving on for. It's dull enough on the ship at any time, but while we are here there is always the possibility of some mail every day. It undoubtedly helps our morale. Major Doran, who came up to the ship yesterday, says that *Dorsetshire* is in Karachi and that Evelyn Cameron is still on her. I hope she is there, when and if we are sent north.

They are coaling today – the awning is down to minimise the coal dust, and the row that is going on, on all sides and below on the barges is indescribable and incredible. There will be no peace anywhere all day. Nickels (IMS) is leaving in a few days to marry Ianto Thomas, who was 3rd mate on this ship, now transferred. He is a dear boy, a general favourite and, being a fellow Cymro, I'm more interested in his welfare. We are all rather staggered and very sorry that this has happened. She's a nice little girl and an extremely pretty one, but, well, I genuinely hope it turns out alright. He is very young and I suppose after all, it's no one's business but his own.

Russia is still holding out magnificently on all fronts, although the winter is settling in.

November 25th 1941

I am writing this in slightly different surroundings – having moved into Nickels' cabin today as she has gone to Calcutta for a few days, prior to finishing altogether and being married. I like it much better than my own in most ways. I have at last got room to put my books out – before I almost had to get on my hands and knees to get them out of the drawers under my bunk.

Well, much has happened in the outside world in the last 100 days, although we remain as static as always. The offensive in Libya has begun in deadly earnest and it is almost certain that Ken is there and not, as I first thought, in the Caucasus. According to all sources we are doing well, having recaptured Bardio and Fort Capuzzo and a garrison from Tobruk which had set out from there to meet up with them. It all sounds terrible and horrible to me and, supposing Ken to be alright, there are always others who are not. I can't help imagining how awful it must be for them, particularly for those who are at all sensitive and there must be so many of them. Of course, I worry and wonder every ten minutes, all day long, although it's silly, I know.

Ken's photograph arrived on Saturday, having been opened by the censor and the customs. I think they must suspect me of some international intrigue! I am delighted with the photograph and I now have more room to display it on my new chest of drawers.

We heard today that our long overdue pay is reposing peacefully in MALAYA. We know that we are marked down for the Far East but whether we shall ever be sent there remains to be seen and depends, I suppose, on whether Japan is bluffing or not. The real reason why they have put us on the Malaya payroll is because we are no longer connected to the Middle East. The Indian Command will not be responsible for Indian rates of pay, even though we've spent the last six months here and the only British rates of pay allocated out here at all are from Singapore. Therefore to save the army a few pounds they have transferred us there. The whole system of pay is perfectly rotten and should be revised, surely. Anyway this is the last straw – nothing paid into the bank for three months and then they send it to Malaya! I made up my mind then and there to ask for a transfer. This is the direct reason for hurrying things along but I have been restless for some time and ever since the Libyan campaign began, only a few days ago, truly, although it seems like years to me already, I have been impatient to get back to the Middle East. It seems a far cry to Libya, as indeed it is. I feel I'd like to be nearer just in case by some miracle we should meet again.

Tonight's news doesn't sound terribly bright; perhaps the first reports were too glowing. Oh dear! How I wish it would end and it's only begun. We are writing out an application for transfer tonight, although I'm sadly afraid that it may have to wait sometime before it transpires, as Evelyn Cameron (from the *Dorsetshire*) and whom we saw today, at the Taj, says she put in for a transfer four months ago and nothing has happened yet. A gloomy prospect indeed. Whilst I was writing this the news began in the bar, and although I wasn't actually listening to it, the words 5th Indian Division fell on my ears, like a blow. I was too late to hear what it was actually about, except that they had captured some desert spot. Now I know for certain that Ken is in this ghastly battle, which they say is still raging – the Germans having brought up fresh planes and troops from without, from Crete and Greece and elsewhere. I must write home now. But I can't think of anything else just now. A letter from Bill this morning, now married. She has been to see General and Miss Williams and is making arrangements to try to see my family. I am so pleased about it.

December 10th 1941

Two days ago Japan declared war, or rather attacked British and American possessions without any warning. Of course we all knew it was possible, even probable, but now that it is actually upon us it comes as a shock just the same. Japan attacked the American fleet in Pearl Harbour, Hawaii, landed troops in Borneo, the Philippines, bombed Hong Kong and Singapore, surrounded Ocean, Swains, Midway and Wake Islands and succeeded in getting Thailand to capitulate – all on the first day. Tonight comes the shattering news that the cruiser *Repulse* (1,200 men) and the battleship *Prince of Wales* (1,500 men), the flagship of the Far East fleet, have been sunk by a Japanese air attack. It is a bitter blow.

How far this is going to affect Australia no one yet knows. I expect the mail may not be so regular anyway. In Libya there have been ups and downs but at the moment the situation is supposed to be satisfactory with two or three isolated out-posts only holding out to the west of Tobruk where we have regained the corridor. 700 New Zealand wounded have been recaptured, much to their delight, I am sure. What an escape!

Russia is holding out magnificently and driving the Germans back on all fronts. How grateful we should feel for allowing us this extra time. What an incredible state of affairs it all is – literally the entire world at war. With what utter inane stupidity mankind has brought about, and has allowed to grow, this dreadful, wanton waste and killing. And I doubt very much if, when it is all over, we shall have learned any valuable lessons from it. The 'inhumanity of man to man makes countless thousands mourn',[42] and so it goes on. I am afraid I feel very bitter about it all. I got so mad at the inane conversation tonight that I picked up my things and departed hence, to my cabin.

No word from Ken and it's over a month now and I suppose it may be as much again and more before I do hear. At times I feel hopeless and despairing that I shall ever see him again. And one can do nothing, absolutely nothing to alter things. That's the maddening part about it. I just walk around this silly deck day after day, listening to Mary tell her oft-repeated tale of one relative or another, until I could scream. The end, alas, seems further off than ever before and there is nothing to do but wait.

The family very kindly sent me £5 for my birthday and Xmas and sister Mona has sent me a collection of really good laces and a draft for £1. Clwyd, I believe, is also sending me a draft. They apparently think I need the money, and how right they are! Still no word about our pay; I should think the Japs will get it before we do.

We have gone well out in mid-stream again after a spell quite near the Gateway. Only three motor boats ashore daily because of petrol rationing.

Mona and I attended a meeting of the recently formed Australian Association of Bombay who hope to raise funds for the general war effort. We also went over to the *Dorsetshire* for tea with Evelyn Cameron on Monday. She takes 750 patients. The *Talamba* is back again, having picked up 400 patients at Suez, Port Sudan, Massawa and Aden. Of course, we still remain static with the decoy ship, the *Centurion*. I'm distinctly fed up tonight. Everyone on the ship annoys me at the present moment. They're uninspiring at any time but tonight – well, they just get under my skin.

December 27th 1941

Christmas day is over and I can easily say thank heaven. I hate these bursts of festivities in the army and besides, I think it is entirely misplaced in a war. We started out with a party at Major Ramchandani's on Xmas Eve. It was a nice party and we enjoyed that. Mona, Hardy and I left at about 9pm and had coffee and sandwiches at the Chinese restaurant and then went on to the cinema. It was a good comedy and at the end we went to the Taj lounge and, over further sandwiches, awaited the hour of the launch's departure. We saw numerous QAs in their grey beiges or grey suits and were congratulating ourselves on not looking like they were, when, to our amazement, in walked Owen and Watson. It was grand seeing them and we made arrangements for them to come onto the ship today. We were very grieved to hear that Hilary Glazebrook had been killed outright in the same accident as Sarah Davidson. I had roomed with them both in London for over three months and they were in Alexandria with us until they went to the Sudan. We felt they were amongst our oldest and best friends. It is all very shocking and even now I can't somehow believe it.

I am hearing from Ken again, so I'm happy. Until yesterday I thought he was in Libya, now I know he is in Cyprus.
It seems I should have heard from Monica (Thompson) about
this but unfortunately the letter has not yet come. The wireless and papers insisted also upon talking about the 5th
Indian Division in Libya and so I was so worried every time
I heard the regiment mentioned. Now for Ken's postscript,
'I still like Cyprus wine', I know that the CO knew what he
was talking about when he told me that the 5th Division
was in Cyprus. I didn't believe it then but now I know he
was right. I am so relieved that Ken is not in Libya and hope
that Cyprus will not prove to be another Crete. I do hope the
poor lamb will get his parcels in time for Xmas; they went
off early enough. Our hampers are presumably on the pile at
HQ where they'll stay until someone throws them out, or it
suits them to change the staff. I am so sick of this ship at
the moment, more particularly of the bridge and Matron and
Scot-White. I could cheerfully push them overboard. It just
annoys me to see them, day after day, sitting in a group on
deck or in the bar, drinking, eternally drinking. If by doing
so they get something out of it, it might be justifiable, but
I've never heard an intelligible remark or an original thought
from any one of them, sober or otherwise.

I have had a letter from home on Christmas Eve and two
fat envelopes containing letters that Clwyd sent home but
nothing from him personally, however, for ages. Oh, and a
delightful surprise in the shape of a parcel from the W to W
campaign – Nurses' Comforts Fund, Victoria. It weighed
nearly 11 pounds and it contained tinned fruit salad, cream,
asparagus, tomato juice, fruit cake, plum pudding, anchovy
and salmon paste, Epson's fruit salts, lamb's wool, powder
puff, talcum powder, toothbrush, lipstick, soap sweets, nuts
and raisins and eau de cologne. I was awfully thrilled to be

specially recognised by an Australian Red Cross Society – we had all been ignored heretofore.

Just this minute we have been informed that we are to move on Monday at 7am and no one knows where. Well, at long last perhaps, we may be able to do something useful.

1942

Bombay – Basrah – Batavia – Colombo – Karachi – Massawa
Bombay – Calcutta, 47th British General Hospital

New Year's Day

And now we are heading for the Persian Gulf, bound for
Basrah! We slid gracefully out of Bombay harbour at 7am last
Monday. Mona and I got up early to wave to Evelyn in the
Dorsetshire as it moved off. Last night, knowing it was useless
to go to bed, we were dragged down to a party in McDonald's
cabin. It was a two-foot squeeze and there must have been
quite twenty of us there. It was hot and dusty and extremely
noisy, to put it mildly, and we thought we could escape after
a modest hour or so. But alas for our guile, we were still there
when someone rang a large brass bell and we gathered round
and sang 'Auld Lang Syne' and everyone kissed everyone else
at midnight. I got down to my cabin about 1am and started a
letter to Ken in Cyprus, where I hope he had a cheerful happy
celebration and didn't think too much. One shouldn't think
too much, I've discovered. Such a nice surprise last night too:

there was a book on my table when I went down at midnight and a letter. It was from Tich, dear Tich, who, although a Hindu, is much more of a Christian than most people I've met in my life. In the note he had written Tagore's lines:

Once we dreamed that we were strangers
We woke up to find that we are dear to each other.

He is a dear little soul. He and Nellie will stand out always as two of the most delightful and loveable people I have ever known – not only among Indians either. Nellie is a Christian, her father being a missionary in an American mission, but Tich is a Hindu and an ardent disciple of Gandhi and a passionate Indian Nationalist or Congressman. Being in the army his style is cramped and he has no bitterness or hatred towards Britain in any case, only a great sadness in his dark eyes that so many millions of his people are starving and that no-one seems to care. I have a deep and abiding sympathy for the peoples of all conquered countries emanating, I suppose, from some remote and woaded ancestor, nearly two thousand years ago.

Well, I am all for India having her independence. It seems all wrong, when we are fighting for so-called democracy, that we can keep virtually enslaved, 400,000,000 people. It wouldn't be so bad if they were an unintelligent race, which they are not, and although they are divided amongst themselves, I believe we have encouraged this for our own ends. At least they should be allowed to work out their own salvation. If we don't give in gracefully, I feel we shall have to pay for it in the end, for this generation is sensitive and proud and ready to defend its independence, come what may. I feel it is only Gandhi's pacifist policy that has kept India in check up to this time. And Gandhi is an old man. His successor may not favour non violence, and it wouldn't take much to fan the fire among 400 million people.

If I do end up living in India I shall have more sympathy with Indians themselves than with most of the British people, who speak so disparagingly of them. I quite despair of there ever being a thousand years of peace when I hear on every side such thoughtless, cruel and unjust criticisms of whole races of people and in their own country. And we think we are more civilised and Christian than any other race. Ah me!

January 10th 1942

Karachi

Basrah is now behind us and 'one with seven thousand years' and we are at Karachi. But to go back a week – it blew up cold through the night about three nights before we reached port. Oh my! We'd forgotten what it was like to feel cold but we soon knew. Out of the bottom of the trunk the warm winter woollies, thick suits and coats, hot water bags, bed socks, winter pyjamas and the rest – things we'd long forgotten we possessed. And then we tied up at Magil about 6pm. The river looked cold and dreary and not so romantic this time – nothing is the second time, so blasé have we become in our roaming around and about. We walked up and down the deck in the hard clear cold air, our teeth literally chattering.

Then Bob arrived and went straight up to the captain, later sending down word to us. Mona and I went ashore with him and picked up Danny at the transport office en route for their house, new, since our last trip there. Mona and Danny went to some official dinner that couldn't be avoided and Bob and I dined at home. It was rather fun and I got four fils[43] pieces out of the Christmas pudding. We went up on to the roof and I wrote my name on the frost on the wall. Oh, bitterly cruelly cold! Then Mona and Danny returned and we played the gramophone until – I was going to say it was dawn – it wasn't far short of it anyway, at 3.30am. I was hung with, there is no other word for it, Bob's enormous navy overcoat, gold epaulettes and all, and eight foot of thick navy blue wool scarf around and around my head. He can have them both – they nearly crushed my spirit completely. It was cold in our bunks and we had only about two hours' sleep at the most, when we had to get up, as the patients arrived at 9am.

We had about 60 boys in C Ward and a grand lot they were: mostly medical cases and up and about with only one or two sick ones. All the asthmatics decided to have attacks to begin with, but once acclimatised settled down nicely. They had a gramophone and we lent them our records as well as Red Cross ones and it was well used from early morning until bedtime. I believe they all enjoyed their cruise and wished it had been longer. They particularly approved of the food (and it was good) and they were allowed to do pretty much as they chose. I don't believe in being officious with patients – it's bad enough to be ill. The cold continued until we were a day off Karachi and we landed everyone intact except one Hindu, whose mortal remains were consigned to the sea a few days out of port. It was a simple ceremony: the guard and the officers and the colonel who attended stood at the salute when the body was sent down the slipway.

We got into Karachi on Saturday about 4pm but the patients did not disembark until Sunday morning. We hated seeing them go, having just got to know one from the other. It's always this way on a ship. Yesterday after tea Katie, Mary and Harold and Mona and I went to town and to the cinema. Looking around for the first time the town seems scattered and provincial, but of course, it was Sunday and all the shops were closed. It may look more businesslike during the week. The weather here is delightful although rather chilly in the shade, but warm and balmy in the sun. We have moved out about 100 yards at most and go to the port in one of the many colourful balham-cum-tonys that congest the little quay; very colourful they are with large red flags in their main masts and scarlet cushions on the seats. They are larger than the Basrah balhams but more after their fashion than the Bombay tonys. No less than five men rowed us across tonight and it cost us a mere two annas a head, so they can't be literally rolling in wealth, although they seem cheerful souls.

The American clipper and the Australian–Dutch airmail sea-planes are moored quite close by. They look retiring and unimportant camouflaged and floating on the tide as they are. Yet what tales they would have to tell if they kept a journal, like me. The docks are interminable, apparently: I certainly can't see the end of them and there are ships of all kinds loading and unloading their various cargoes. But it is the numerous and varied fishing craft and native sailing boats that lend colour and atmosphere to the little harbour one way or another – especially after our mail begins to arrive. We feel we shall like Karachi; it's odd to think that we now know such places as Basrah and Alexandria and Bombay and Karachi – which before were only names.

The gong has just gone. I have retired to bed early, having a cold and not wanting dinner. It's nice to be alone for a while – it seems impossible on this ship, short of being rude to everybody and locking myself in my cabin.

January 23rd 1942

On deck in the sun. The weather is still delightful, some days rather coolish in the shade but whenever we have been ashore, it has been almost too hot. The nights remain deliciously cool, however, which is sheer heaven after Bombay. Here as I write the gulls wheel and turn and fly about us. Hundreds of river craft – fishing and cargo – with beautiful curled sails, large ones and tiny ones, go up and down every hour of the day and late into the night. More graceful and lovelier than a dream these sailing boats and long after Karachi has become blurred in my memory the little butterfly boats will remain. But directly opposite, about 300 yards from us, is the wharf, or rather the beginning of it, for it seems to go on forever, as far as the eye can see.

Daily, fairly large ships come and, within 24 hours, are gone again. Mostly cargos from all appearances, but sometimes, as today, long lines of troops embark, quickly and silently and go their ways. The flying boats, too, arrive and depart, usually at night. And how skilfully they are handled by their pilots landing on the water, at length, and in the pitch darkness (except for their own lights) with scarcely a ripple or splash. Yet we accept our airmail without question or thanks and merely complain when our mail is overdue. So much do we consider these feats as part of our desserts in these advanced days!

Karachi we find more or less adequate for our needs although more expensive than Bombay. I have had a red dress made. I've wanted a red winter frock for a long time now and I've got it. The colour is more or less what I wanted but the tailor has not turned out to be quite the best although we went to the best-looking shop in the place. I've bought myself some shoes too, wine ones and being English, K shoes. I had to pay Rs28 and so for the remainder of the month I go penniless. Well we can't have it both ways and really I don't need anything. We managed to get Rs100 from the field cashier a few days after we arrived and are simply awaiting the first of next month to collect the same again and more if possible.

We've been into town several times to the pictures and dinner afterwards. There isn't anywhere we can eat except Chinese restaurants. Actually they are clean and cheerful with scarlet screens and scarlet Vs all round and about, which amuses one at first and then doesn't! The food is good but one gets fed up with noodles and prawns and such, or ham and eggs – not that it matters really. We went out on two occasions with Harold and two of his engineer friends, nice ones, a Scot and one from Liverpool. We had a few tense moments on India's behalf but it passed off quite well, eventually. Those moments!

We've had some mail but to my mind not nearly all we should have had. I had about ten letters on two successive days, last week. Nothing since. Mother's appear to be up to date and there was one from Edna, Clwyd and Mona and various others. But only one from Ken. I can't quite understand this as his letters should be getting through quite well.

Yesterday came the bad news that New Guinea was threatened with an invasion and that Rabaul has had several full-scale air attacks. This morning I got myself up in time for the 8.15am news to hear that Rabaul had been silent since 4pm yesterday. No wireless communication at all. So that, I suppose, is that. The idea is of course to use New Guinea as a base from which to attack Australia. And one wonders, now, with all the air reverses everywhere, how they are to be stopped from getting their objective. Oil supplies have been cut off between America and the ME and even from Borneo and the East Indies now, where they have had to destroy them – and communications are difficult generally anywhere between the Far East and Australia. I am wondering of course about Clwyd and whether he is still there or back in Australia again. I expect that they will be frantic at home, although as long as he does escape successfully I expect he won't mind at all, being involved for the moment. It's rather ironic that Clwyd, with his pacifist principles and his seemingly safe job for the duration – although it just happened that way – should really be the first one to be involved. I couldn't hear the news this midday, which is extremely irritating with all this going on – so I don't know whether the Japs have met with resistance or not. One wonders how, where and when it will all end. Fantastic to think that of all countries anywhere, the eyes of the world are on Australia.

February 4th 1942

Onward bound from Colombo [44] to Batavia

We stepped out of the harbour about 8am this morning and now with Singapore as our first goal, we are en route for Batavia.[45] We left Karachi on the morning of the 27th of January – a Wednesday I think – and we were told of it the afternoon of the previous Monday. We had more or less made up our minds that Karachi was to be our spiritual home henceforth, instead of Bombay, and when the news came that we were off again and this time to the FAR EAST, we could scarcely believe it. We did some quick thinking, and as it was the end of the month and there was no field cashier in Colombo, we decided to storm the citadel and ask for our next month's pay in advance. Scotty and Wright between them worked the oracle and lo and behold we each collected Rs150 with no bother at all. Now at long last there was a gentleman amongst field cashiers – a rare specimen indeed and as such, to be revered and treasured against another such rainy day – in Karachi. So of course we dashed into town in fine frenzy, in the train – our usual means of transport when alone, five pies (paise)[46] from Keamari into town (about 8 miles) as against five rupees in a taxi! There we squandered a lot of our newly acquired subsistence but only, actually, on essential things.

We took a victoria back to the docks – Mary, Mona and I packed around with purchases and we set off behind a hefty looking horse and a charming gentleman in a fly, who knew no English. We got on splendidly until we reached the bridge at the Port Trust building, and then the old horse decided he'd prefer to turn around and head for home and no amount of coaxing, threats, slashes from the whip or invocations to Allah would persuade him to do otherwise. Of course the usual interested crowd gathered around to admire and advise – the horse was nearly in the victoria with us, by this time of course – and we ended up letting him go his own sweet way, which was about a mile back along the way we had come, and then either for reasons sentimental or temperamental, which we shall never know alas, he went suddenly down a side road and, by some miracle, arrived at the docks and delivered us safe and sound. Quite exciting and all for Rs2! That was our last excursion ashore in Karachi and when we got back there was mail for me, one from Mother, Mona and Ken (I had had one from Bob just before going out).

Ken's letter had been written on Xmas day so it took long enough to arrive. He was annoyed that I wasn't getting all his letters, and I know I am not, and they are taking so much longer to arrive than ever before. Well, it was lovely to hear from them all at the eleventh hour, because I expect it will be four or five weeks before we collect our next mail. What a day that will be. So much happens in a few weeks these days. I quite expect that I'll hear in my next letter from home that Clwyd has been evacuated. I am so pleased that they all received their little odds and ends at Christmas but the wretched skin condition of mother's still continues to worry her.

Rabaul is apparently still in Japanese hands and we hear that Port Moresby has been bombed. Since we left Karachi we have been completely news-less (except for odd snips that we are not supposed to hear from 'Sparks'). All wireless sets, private and otherwise, have to be handed in because of vibrations! This seems perfectly ridiculous in a hospital ship that sails at night, ablaze with lights and is supposed to be more or less neutral in any case. Since leaving Colombo the captain, after a struggle, has obtained permission for us to use one general set to which everyone must listen if he wishes to hear the news. We got into Colombo – five years exactly since I went through here in 1937[47]– at about 8.30am on Monday morning and we had 48 hours there. Coaling took us longer than we first thought because it appears that there is a good deal of labour shortage, hereabouts. The harbour was chock-a-block with ships' cargo, amid merchantmen (P&O), corvettes,[48] destroyers, cruisers (*Cornwall* and *Slogav*), troop carriers, tankers and all manner of ocean going craft.

They told us that there were 75 big ships in, all at the same time. What a target for the Japanese planes, if they only knew. In the morning, while Mona was on deck, an Australian Red Cross man came up to her and asked if she was one of the two Australians aboard and, learning she was, asked her to go and see them when we went ashore. We did and they were charming to us and most kind. The head of the whole Red Cross in Colombo is a man called Wilkinson, an old Wesley boy, and such a nice man. He told us that there was no British Red Cross at all and the Australian bunch acted for all and sundry and very generously and efficiently too, I should say. They gave us a hamper each, such as they give to their own boys and sisters. McConachi was the name of the other man and he was a cousin of the family in Queenscliffe where, I know, my family have stayed at least once.

While we were there the matron of the 12th Australian Hospital came in and she asked us to go out to dinner to the hospital and it was arranged that we accompany Major Perry (Melbourne) and two New South Walians. It was a delightful drive out to the hospital – about eight miles – on a road similar to the Kandy Road, green banana and coconut palms growing thickly on either side and lush green grass and undergrowth to the very road's edge. Hibiscus, frangipani, oleander and bougainvillea were a riot of colour everywhere and once again we met the quaint straw-covered bullock-drawn carts, rickshaws and the Singhalese men with their long hair coiled in a neat bun on the back of their heads. The sari isn't worn so much or with such variety of colour and fabric as in Bombay but I did see some rather lovely girls.

The hospital itself reminded me of the hospital in Geelong, although it is larger and covers more acres of ground. The wards are built bungalow-style with red roofs and walls that finish half way to the ceiling. Wide verandas keep the weather out and individual mosquito nets, somehow suspended from the ceiling, dissuade the local mosquitoes and their brethren from disturbing the minister in his bed o' nights. Long pillared covered ways connect the wards and wide strips of green grass divide them. The Sisters' Mess and quarters are most attractive. They introduced us to lots of the girls – they looked so nice en bloc in their grey frocks and red capes and we felt so inferior in our white drill overalls and white stockings and shoes. I met Rae and Vickers (Victoria), the latter, it appears, was at Bonegillia hospital near Melbourne with sister Mona. She has just had a photograph sent to her of the staff there at present and there, sure enough in the back row, was 'our Mona'. Well, well, a small world. The girls plied us with questions and seemed quite awed and impressed with our very ordinary experiences. It's odd that we never think of ourselves as being 'interesting'; one grows accustomed to seeing fresh fields every few weeks. A pity perhaps.

After dinner we had a most delightful concert out o'doors under a full moon, sitting on deckchairs on the lawn. The MOs have formed a musical society and one of them, Bolebatch, who compiled the programme, gave a brief but comprehensive sketch of the composer and the circumstances in which the composition was written – or the story, if it was an opera. In the first half, records of *La Bohème* and Gounod's *Funeral March of a Marionette* and other familiar modern things were played. In the second half, the whole score of the ballet *The Firebird*. It was really heavenly to hear some good music again. After that we went up to the mess and sitting outside, had supper – tea and sandwiches and homemade cakes (a real Australian tea!) and there was more talk again about one another. The whole evening was a series of 'Do you knows?' and 'Do you remember?' Two of the MOs drove us back to the Red Cross and came down with us to the wharf to see us onto the launch all set for *Karapara*. It had been a most pleasant and exciting day, because so unexpected. And I believe the people whom we met were quite delighted to meet new Australians again. We quite hope that we shall call here often and will be certain of good friends while the 12th Australian hospital and the Red Cross are here.

Next morning we were allowed ashore leave until midday and, clad in clean white overalls, we set out in the BI launch for the shore. Just as we reached the steps, I got the full force of the back wash, and as the whole harbour was literarily covered in filthy black oil, discharged the previous day from a tanker that had been torpedoed ten miles off, and which had been towed into Colombo with a lovely hole right through her amidships, I was a sight to behold! From my shoulders to my waist I was a mass of oil and there were splashes of it, alas, on my white hat, shoes and stockings, bag and kid gloves. Oh dear! Well, everyone was very upset and it was nobody's fault and there was nothing to be gained by sitting weeping about it, so I steeled myself from thinking about what I must look like from the rear and proceeded into town and did my shopping as though I was still attired in spotless white. It was rather an ordeal but such things can be done as long as one makes up one's mind that there is no alternative.

We didn't sail yesterday, however, as we had first thought, but we are 'on our lawful occasions' now, well out to sea (the gong has just gone at 1pm) and once again there is no land to be seen anywhere at all.

It all seems rather peaceful like any summertime cruise and it seems also quite incredible that we are on our way to the Dutch East Indies.[49] Singapore, of course, is now a fortress, all our troops having withdrawn to the island, and it is being bombed relentlessly according to all the news. Time will tell whether we shall really get there. We get our orders in Batavia, it appears. The *Talamba* 'got in alright' and away again with her patients and they dropped the Australian lads in Colombo although the ship was en route for Karachi. Maybe we'll all do the same. This time, just five years ago, I was on the old *Mongolia* outward bound for England. Well, a lot of water has flowed under the bridge in five years and the face of the world has altered quite considerably. Now I'm heading towards Australia – the north of it this time – and very near it too I expect in a week's time, but just as far away as ever in terms of touching it. The airmail is now suspended which removes the strongest link of all and I shall miss my faithful weekly bulletin from Mama and I expect she will miss mine. I expect most of them will arrive eventually but in sixes and sevens as General's have done for so long.

This morning I packed an emergency bag in case of 'abandon ship' – two actually: one with essentials such as toothbrush, soap, towel, cream and powder, sun glasses, passport and cheque book and so on; the other with as much of my new undies as I can stuff in and which I have no intention of resigning to the fishes. I shouldn't mind losing my uniforms at all but I should hate to lose my entire gradually acquired mufti. Not that I even think that we shall ever need these bags, but in case of such an eventuality, I should only have to grab them and run!

And now, my recording up to date, I am all set for my afternoon sleep which has become habitual, I fear.

February 9th 1942

Far East NE1

I am waiting for the bath boy to tell me my bath is ready. Only half a tub these days because we are conserving water! Oh! The sea and sky tonight! As I look up through my porthole and reflected also in my wall mirror, there is a bank of cloud of the deepest violet, shot through and through with palest rose. Above it the sky is turquoise and apricot; below, where it meets the sea on the horizon, an ever deepening flame. The sea is smooth as silk, except for a deep swell, and the colour of it is like all the opals of the entire world. It's a pity I'm so inarticulate because tonight I feel like Turner and Keats and Beethoven all rolled into one. Yet we are told, only two days away from us is bitter fighting, an incredible thought indeed. The news announces that the Japanese have landed forces in Singapore and that Java expects an attack at any time. Maybe even yet we may receive an order to turn round and go home. Hateful thought: so far we have not done anything really useful and none of us can bear the thought of turning back at this stage. Meanwhile we are on our way – and I go to my bath!

Later

We arrived in the outer harbour of Batavia in the early afternoon. The CO and the captain went ashore in a colourful little mine-sweeper for orders. It seems, as usual, no-one knew we were coming or even what we were. We were put on eight hours sailing and thereupon settled ourselves for the night. It was a broken one, however, for an air raid siren went at 1.15am and, reluctantly, we crawled out of our bunks and got into some clothes and a tin hat in total darkness and foregathered as pre-instructed along the corridor. We sat on our lifebelts for extra comfort, listened to fatuous remarks from the matron, who always, for some obscure reason, feels she has to entertain the company assembled. After about two hours of it, the CO allowed us to return to our cabins on the condition that we did not undress. The all clear did not sound until 7.15am although it seems there was nothing in it from beginning to end as far as we could tell. The previous night we got up at 2am to see Krakatoa looming blackly on our portside, but to all intents and purposes, asleep and disinterested. We passed numerous small islands, dotted here and there, all thickly covered with trees and vegetation – some very tiny indeed. I thought I'd like to buy one, a completely uninhabited one, and retire there at weekends, when I'm suffering from a superfluity of irritations brought on by careless, stupid wild talk against which I seem to wage unceasing war.

We all went down to our cabins after lunch intent on making up for last night's thwarted slumbers, but we suddenly moved off at 5pm and came alongside. We were told that a cruiser was bringing in some patients and that probably we should have them on board tonight. And just as the dinner gong was sounding, there came an armed merchant cruiser *Durban*, which had run the gauntlet of 27 attacking planes from Singapore; they had received two bombs and missed the other 170. Nine of the crew were killed and we got the remaining 13, about ten of whom are very badly wounded.

Mona and Mary stayed for a while and then Scotty retired to theatre, where she still is at 3am and is likely to remain until daylight or until the dressings run out. Major Ramchandani and Parnan, half the BORs, MacDonald, Kitto and various others are still about. In spite of the entire disturbance some of the boys are managing to sleep, from sheer exhaustion, I suppose. They all have the same tale – it must be absolute hell in Singapore. There are conflicting stories as to whether the hospitals are still there, although it seems the 13th AGH has had several bombs anyway. There are two RAF POs in for the night, both Australians – one, it seemed, worked in Fords, Geelong, and used to live in Pryce Street! Unfortunately, there is a tale going about that some AIF 'jumped the b------' and manned the Tommy guns. And McDonald made me indignant tonight by telling me that he's been told on the usual 'good authority' that the Australians weren't fighting at all well in Singapore and that they'd 'let us down badly'. Of course, I flayed him for repeating such idle, stupid and loose talk.

If only people would realise the harm of such words. If we can't have unity and better manners and kinder feelings among people of the same race, it's a poor outlook for the ultimate end of this bloody business. I feel so cross about this. Tomorrow I expect we'll have some of those same AIFs here and, these tales having circulated in advance of their arrival, I rather fear the consequences. I hate all this childishness among grown people. It seems we may be here for some time; probably acting as a base and taking all the odds and ends of wounded that will drift in here from day to day. Once we have our complement we shall depart, I suppose, and we hope it will be soon.

The harbour is full of ships, near in and far out, and flying boats seem as 'thick as leaves in Vallombrosa'.[50] As I write there are planes buzzing about but I presume they are Dutch and British as so far there has been no alarm.

I must finish this now. Oh, we walked for about 15 minutes on the docks this evening, just to get the feel of Java under our feet. Alas, Batavia is five miles inland and it seems a 'forbidden city' to us. I'd like to come here again, years hence when all is quiet again.

February 15th 1942

I had a good sleep today and here I am holding the fort again. We have our full complement of patients now and more, every bed is full and some are on mattresses on the floor. It's an indescribable scene, with BORs and brigadier generals all sleeping gloriously and indiscriminately alongside each other.

To do the officers justice, they accept it all very pleasantly and so far there has been no murmur of dissent. Of course, this is only the first day and complaints may crop up in due course. There are some very sick men in B Ward and we are still sending cases to theatre at midnight. It's finished for tonight, I hope, although they will be at it again in the morning. There are a considerable number of Australians among them, liberally distributed in all the wards, and many of the Indian wards are almost entirely Australian. I've been greeted tonight with all the good natured chaff about that much maligned stream, the Yarra, but they seem pleased to know that there was someone more or less belonging to them on board.

We sail, it is said, about 7am and we shall all be mighty glad to be at sea again. The blackout at night is depressing and having the ports closed in those crowded wards doesn't improve the already rather awful atmosphere. Almost every case of the 360 is surgical, either wounds or plasters, and often both. I imagine that we have every conceivable known variety of splint and plaster cast, a more motley unshaven grimy assembly it would be difficult to imagine. I do imagine that there will still be some having their first wash when we reach Colombo, that is, if the water supply hangs out that far. There are two Australians in the padded cells, one homicidal and the other suicidal, and neither will eat or drink or allow anyone to come near him. It is dreadful to think that these two men were sane and normal when they left home and that having been through the hell of this war, they probably will never be so again. And there will be hundreds, perhaps thousands more of them before it is all over. It is just too ghastly to think about. We have been told that there are 60,000 troops to be evacuated from Singapore and if 5,000 can be got away they will be fortunate. This may well be exaggerated but I expect it is a grim story at best. The *Empire Star* came alongside early this morning. Among the troops there were RAF wives and children and a number of AIF Sisters, some Dutch ones and at least one QA.

Those who have been at Narvik and Dunkirk say that Singapore is the worst of all. Talking with the second mate over the rails this morning at 3am we have decided that it is all too grim for words and still the wireless continues to soft-soap the public and say that all is being done and that indeed this is just what we had planned. Apparently, the government believes that the public is possessed of a very low intelligence, if it cannot see through the padding and the inane and fatuous statements uttered daily on air and in the press.

February 16th 1942

4am

I have just returned to the lounge after doing rounds. I must walk miles these nights and my feet feel like it – up stairs and companionways, scrabbling in and out between beds in C Ward. I've just had to go down to F Ward for some astringent as no other ward possessed any and that is about ten miles at least, I should say. I always saw to the dispensary myself in C Ward and although I've made a song about it each morning, A and B are quite hopeless with theirs so the result is that I am always borrowing. We took in a colonel from Surgery tonight after they had done his leg in theatre: compound tibia and fibula and a really filthy enormous wound; it is not in plaster and slung up in a cock-up splint and extension. I've given four lots of morphia at least and various 2/15ths and 3/15ths and so on in an effort to induce them to sleep. Most of them are asleep now actually, but a few are restless, still fighting the Japs mentally, I suppose.

There is a lot of criticism, so the wireless reports, about the escape to a home port of three large German battleships, which is to lead to the navy and army having their own air-arms. Singapore they are lamenting, but telling themselves that it isn't as bad as when France fell. If the general public only knew the mess that was and is Singapore and all the bitterness and criticism on these boys' lips, they might think twice before talking so glibly about necessary sacrifices on the altar of their arrogance and pride. Everyone is unanimous that there is and never was any organisation in Singapore and that, since we are going to lose it eventually, it should have been evacuated long before, and most of the men saved. But, of course, we had our 'prestige' to consider.

February 17th 1942

3.30am

So Singapore has surrendered unconditionally and 60,000 troops are left behind. It's all very sad and depressing. From Batavia came the announcement that some town in Java had been occupied by the Japanese and an important airdrome in Sumatra has gone. We have landed some troops – Australian and American – in Java. I am wondering if my sister Mona will be sent there. If Java goes then one shudders to think of the consequences for India and Australia.

I've more theatre cases this evening. For some reason best known to themselves they begin operating at 8pm these days. I've complained about it as it disturbs my patients when they need to sleep. I hope it is the last night of this nonsense. More annoying innuendoes from Matron this morning. She announced to Mona in front of the patients – 'there's an Australian throwing his food around and he's going to see the colonel'. The food is very poor indeed on this trip so he's justified. She loves to make a point of his being an Australian – a very low breed they must be – and if there is any trouble anywhere it's always one of my much maligned fellow countrymen who is to blame. I feel so resentful and irritated when I hear Matron's remarks. Why she joined the QAs, I can't think; it certainly wasn't for the love of, or pity for, suffering humanity. She's about as low and ignorant as any form of animal life and we realise it's not worth getting upset on her behalf, although it does get under my skin.

February 18th 1942

5.30pm

Another night gone and we get to Colombo on Sunday morning, so it is said. After that, popular rumour has it that we go on to Bombay. I hope we do, if it is only for mail. I haven't the slightest doubt that wherever we are sent we shall be told that our mail has 'just been sent' to Colombo or Karachi or Timbuktu. A few more years like this and I shall be resigned to anything. I can understand the British character better now with its general lethargy and apathy; their resistance has been worn down by years of inefficiency. And even when you are hopeful and sanguine by nature, it gradually wears you down in time. You find yourself either resigned or bitter, perhaps both.

February 21st 1942

1.45am

Two days ago we had a little untoward excitement. I was about to go down to bed at about 9.30 when I noticed a crowd on deck gazing ardently over the rails and I discovered that a patient had decided to jump overboard. We still don't know if he wanted to drown or just go for a swim. He jumped deliberately anyway and it was too late for anyone to get him. Someone threw him a lifebelt and they stopped the ship in one and a half minutes! A boat was lowered after some time but it was scarcely necessary as he continued to swim about quite merrily in his pyjamas and shoes and he had almost caught up with the ship again before they picked him up. I believe he was quite non-committal and said merely that he didn't have a long enough swim. It really was funny to watch him swimming so easily in mid-ocean and to all intents and purposes enjoying it. Fortunately it was calm and there were no sharks. It caused quite a stir of course and the colonel was flapping about with the result that all anxiety neurosis patients, however sane, have been placed under guard if not lock and key since.

Darwin has been bombed twice. In fact we don't seem to be doing anything to redress the situation, anywhere. The Russians, alone, appear to be pushing on. We have heard from everyone that the Japs have been particular everywhere to respect hospitals – in each case giving ample warning for them to evacuate their patients. It's rather surprising in the light of the Chinese atrocities, but it seems to be true nevertheless. The patients here have more or less settled down and everything is under control now. No one is really ill in C Ward, and then the only DIL patient has been transferred to B today, so I can keep an eye on him better at night. Carrol, my night orderly, is such a good boy and nice with the patients. The nights pass quickly enough generally speaking. First one then another comes along for a chat over the rails, the major, then Edwards (4th) after his watch, then Harold soon after 4am and Clarke (2nd). I start work soon after 5am and the time goes quickly then. But it is still very sticky and warm and there is lightning every night. One more night and then Colombo!

February 23rd 1942

Colombo to Bombay

We left at 3am today. Yesterday we disembarked all Dominion troops and all naval personnel to the Australian hospital. The harbour was crowded with ships, many of them packed with troops which we found out were Australians. It seems they are leaving the ME and returning en masse either to Java or Australia. Paso Pengharen, whom we met in Alexandria, came aboard this morning, looking for us and it was he who gave us the news that everyone was heading for home again. I expect Padre Helman and Bill Williams and Ted and many more of my old Alexandria friends are among them. A pity to miss them. We have many empty beds now so the nights seem easy, or would be except that Colonel Churcher insists on sending up for me every half hour or so. However, I've tried him on paraldehyde tonight and I am hoping for results. Twenty letters came aboard it seems, but none for us. The second mate has produced another book for me to continue my narrative – so here endeth the first!

March 11th 1942

Karachi

And so beginneth the second volume. We have been here ten days and so far there has been no sign of any movement on our part, or the *Tyrrhea*'s, and with the Far East almost a memory it would seem that there is nothing left for us to do now, except perhaps an odd trip to Basrah.

The latest inhabitants (European) have been exceedingly kind to us hereabouts. We were invited to dinner with a Mr and

Mrs Cullen, who took us on later to the dance at the Garrison Hall. They were really very charming and we enjoyed ourselves – particularly so at their house, I think; although the dance was inclined to be a rough and tumble as the night wore on.

There is little to record since we arrived here nearly three weeks ago: an odd dinner here and there, tea or a picnic as when we went to Sandspit beach on Saturday afternoon with the McLashens (Port Trust). Mostly we stay on board and amuse ourselves as best we can. The main mail has still not arrived. I'd hate to pollute this page with my sentiments regarding the Sea Transport! I haven't heard from home or from Ken for about seven weeks and it seems like years. But I had an interesting letter from Mali and no fewer than three packets of books and magazines, including Charles Morgan's latest *The Empty Room*, Somerset Maugham's *The Gentleman in the Parlour* and *The Road to Bordeaux* by Denis and Cooper. I also received several *John O'London's* and a copy of *Horizon* and *Life and Letters Today.* Lovely! Apart from these, and a solitary letter from Bob, there is nothing. I fume and fume about it and then descend into a mood of utter despair and resignation. It seems so hopeless trying to get any sense or satisfaction out of any government department in these days; they were always bad and entangled with red tape but now they are worse than ever.

No word from Delhi yet. I can see that my next move is to write to Miss Jones. Unfortunately the letters take so long to get through, even one way. One loses heart before one begins and yet that way lies defeat but I must do something about it. If I never benefit from it, at least I can insist on getting some satisfaction before I finish with the QAs. The IMS girls have just had 200 chips refunded to them for messing allowances. We've never seen 200 chips at once in all our lives and no pay at all since last August. Now it seems the CO Malaya has arrived in Australia with his money and papers. Well, bless him for that, anyway. Now I presume we'll begin to be paid from Darwin and the ships take about two months or more to arrive with mail, so that'll be grand. What doesn't go down to the fish may possibly reach us, if we live long enough.

I expect to hear any day now that Port Moresby has had a full scale attack and I expect that Mother is worrying dreadfully about Clwyd. But of course I get no letters and I know nothing of what is happening anywhere. Sir Stafford Cripps is on his way to India to try and settle the deadlock between India and Britain. I hope he's successful.

April 9th 1942

On deck – Basrah!

Over a month in Karachi and here we are in Basrah once again. It was the usual static existence whilst we were in Karachi but pleasant weather and an occasional excursion into town helped the time to pass quickly enough. We went to a garden party at Government House one afternoon; we in our beautiful white drills and the rest superbly attired in garden party frocks and the ever lovely sari. I still have a vision of those Indian women in a hundred different colours walking across the cool green lawns. The gardens were lovely too – petunias, phlox, antirrhinums, dahlias and salpiglossis and so many other old favourites. How heavenly to walk in a garden after so many months aboard a ship.

Then one day we went out in mid-stream, some distance out. The *Georgie* was being towed in and, as she was so large – the largest ship ever to come into Karachi – we had to move out. She had been badly bombed off Suez some months ago and was towed by tugs all the way. She looked enormous as she went in, quite dwarfing all the other ships near her.

We quite thought we were going back into Karachi, but as we were anticipating orders to move, we received instead word to go on to Bombay. This shook us rather badly and more especially because it was the beginning of the month and we had not seen the field cashier. Of course there is one in Bombay but we only got Rs115 from him while the Karachi allowance is more generous, allowing us Rs150 or more. Having reconciled ourselves to this, we suddenly received a signal to tell us to proceed to Basrah – about 36 hours out. As we had no stores on board for patients, we had to put out into Karachi for 24 hours to replenish stores. It was Easter weekend but we had managed to get Rs50 from the FC and that sufficed temporarily. The *Dorsetshire* was in too so we saw Evelyn once again: we went over one evening and they came over for coffee the last morning. Now we are in Basrah, alongside. We arrived early this morning and leave tomorrow morning.

Bob came on board about 11am and later sent up the most gorgeous flowers. Real flowers, fresh and fragrant from the garden. Perfectly lovely. He came and had lunch with me later as the CO would not allow me off the ship for tiffin. The patients started arriving soon after 2pm and were still coming in ones and twos until almost 7pm. I am in Officers and Sick BORs this time. We were full except for four beds in Officers. Bob and Danny came again in the evening after we had handed over to Mary who was doing night duty. Poor Danny looked so sad and changed with reasons enough for that matter. Bob was – well, Bob! Duncan and Murphy completed the party and it was a long session and not altogether pleasing to some of us. But it couldn't be helped and we couldn't walk out for any apparent reason.

We left next morning early. It was a pleasant trip up the Gulf. We all had a delightful lot of boys, very quiet and orderly and there were no complaints. I lost one man, sad to relate; he was too ill to have been moved actually, although as he probably would have died in any case, I fancy he was better off on the ship than in the last hospital, where he had been, in Libya. He wasn't buried at sea, which is unusual but they took him ashore, covered with the flag, as soon as we berthed at Karachi and he was to be buried there by a Roman Catholic padre. I've written to his wife.

I've been desperately tired lately, not physically, so much as mentally. I wonder if I shall remember all this when I read these words, many years hence. Maybe I shall smile then, although I didn't feel much like it at the time.

April 22nd 1942

Jimmy's birthday today. There was the usual party before lunch. Inescapable.

April 23rd 1942

Went into town by taxi and took Kevin with us. He was on his way to see Mary, who is in the BMH, having trouble with a tooth. It seems she took the second anaesthetic very badly and they didn't do anything in the end. She doesn't realise it but she stopped breathing on the table and they were very worried about her for a while. Jenny and I booked seats for *No, No Nannette* and then went for a drive to Clifton. Quite nice there – a long colonnade and steps to the sea somewhere beyond; trim little enclosed gardens on each side and when the zinnias are in bloom it should be colourful. To the Sym Chat and then, and while we were there, Matron and Captain Raj walked in, so we sat together until it was time for us to leave for dinner. We went back to the Grand and then walked to the Paradise in the cool evening air. The picture was fairly good but not particularly so.

Then a gharry home with the hood down. I always like going back to Keamari town with the clip clop of the horses' feet, the still cool starry night, all unhurried and peaceful and the bunder setting off from the little harbour over the still black waters. Sometimes, as last night, there is a golden path from the moon and white sails crossing it. All the big ships are blacked out except for port and starboard lights and there is no sound at all except for the splash of the oar, if there isn't enough wind to allow the sail to take us along. Lately, during the day, it would have been rather too boisterous. Coming back at midday two days ago, we nearly went over as we turned out of the basin. A very nasty moment. I shall remember these things perhaps, when I am far from here: the boatmen, or bunder-wallahs, usually one man and perhaps two small boys. Often the 'man at the wheel' is a boy aged not more than six years old and he brings us alongside as easily as anything. And shinning up the great tall masts and standing aloft with only their toes curling around a rope is a feat of no mean order.

April 29th 1942

Karachi to Basrah

We heard last Friday that we were to set out again for Basrah on Sunday. Only half an hour before I had had a letter from Bob saying he was coming to Karachi on leave. And then this news. I feel so sorry, visualising the poor man in a strange town knowing no-one and all of us departed. The launch came in next day and a note with it to say that he saw no release until the end of the month and that he would be probably coming by plane. So maybe it'll be alright after all.

We had Matron, Cameron and Mona for tea one day. I fear that they will have left before we return and if so – and if they go to the Middle East – they will not be returning. Mary is back with us, but is not doing duty this trip. Scotty and Matron are being childish about the wards and I'm fed up with both of them coming to me with much be-twisted stories of what each said to the other and so forth. For grown women these two ought to be ashamed of themselves.

It's getting warmer and stickier but it could be worse. Quite a lot of rocky coastline yesterday and odd ships. We are supposed to get in sometime tomorrow I think, but time will tell.

I'm finishing my mats at long last and, with other odds and ends of sewing and an occasional letter or air-graph, the day passes somehow. The evenings, in part, we have spent usually sewing, while Jimmy reads us his favourite Elizabethan poets. I am trying to introduce an occasional modern work but it doesn't seem to go down too well. Well, it's as good a way of passing the evenings as any and better than most. And if I don't want to listen, I can just let my mind drift as it often does, from one thing to another and from one country to another.

No more letters, of course; no cable from home either. It is possible to go on week after week without mail, although I once thought it impossible. Perhaps I shall acquire patience at long last. Perhaps.

Poor Ken in his sandy desert. How he must loathe it. Nearly ten months since I saw him and maybe it'll be another ten, twenty, thirty more until I do. Well, I won't think … I won't think at all.

June 21st 1942

Port Sudan – en route for Massawa

Night duty. Hot as hot and sticky as ever was!

But soft – I find it nearly two months since I wrote herein. Well Basrah came and went, or rather we did. We arrived in the early morning and Bob came aboard during that morning and we embarked the patients during the afternoon. I had all Indians in C Ward, with the exception of about 16 BORs. I managed to get them all taped and in their beds and was off duty about 9pm when Bob came back with some gorgeous flowers and, just as an afterthought as it were, a wireless set. After a considerable struggle – for and against – it was decided at length that it should remain. I may add here that it has given us all a new lease of life and the evenings pass in a flash nowadays. We feel we are in touch with the outside world once again and it's lovely to hear music – music! Bob told us of his plan to spend his leave in Karachi and that he proposed to fly to save time.

The trip back was pleasant and my Indian patients were delightful. With about six good words and true of Hindustani, I managed to pull them through all right until we reached port, at least. All sorts and ranks of Sikhs, that handsome race – Madrasees[51], Punjabis, Ghurkhas and a good-humoured, well-mannered, innocent collection of men including sweepers, dhobis, Indian hospital staff, chefs, potato peelers and havildars.[52] Such friendly flashing smiles, no complaints and a great deal of patience. I was most happy amongst them. No meals to bother about either as their two settings of curry and rice were mysteriously supplied to them somewhere for'ard. I never found out just where, but as they looked satisfied and didn't complain, I presume they got what they wanted. We disembarked them after the usual five-day trip, and in the evening Bob arrived, having left by plane at 2am that morning. A long tiring trip. He stayed at the H. Singh club for the first few days and then got a nice room at the Killarney. He was there for seventeen days during which we saw him daily. It was marvellous not to have to resort to the front seat of the always overcrowded train en route for Karachi. Then out of the blue, as it were, the blow fell: we were to leave next day for Basrah. Bob was going back by ship in a few days time but decided to fly back instead.

June 22nd 1942

Basrah again and very hot – it being the summer of the year. And there on the wharf – in the flesh – and I think possibly to the amazement of the bridge and the personnel in general, was that man again!

Whilst Cairo and Baghdad were tossing signals back and forth to each other as to whether we should return to Karachi with patients from Baghdad or take on the 58th IMS and their equipment and carry them to the ME, we were in Basrah for six days. It was delightful for Mona and me to be able to go ashore and have lunch with Bob and Danny at their bungalow. We stayed there whilst they went back to the office at 4pm and had a sleep and a bath and remained for dinner. They have always been incredibly good to us whenever we've been thereabouts. We left and in due course arrived in Aden where we coaled and Mona and I went ashore to do some shopping, *comme il faut*.

On our return, and to our astonishment, there was mail on board. Quite by accident, naturally – all our mail arrives by accident – and never by first intention, I had 24 letters and some papers from Mali. Among them were letters from Mother and eight from General. So most of Mother's missing mail is now received and I can now piece the story together of Clwyd's and Glyn's movements of recent months. On our way early next morning and, after wilting languidly in a perpetual swathe of perspiration through the Red Sea, we arrived in Suez early one morning (16th or 17th). I had quite thought there was no chance of getting in touch with Ken, because I found I had previously sent his address to Mother, thinking I had another, and moreover, I had no idea where he was, except somewhere in the Canal Zone.

We were allowed ashore after 4pm and nothing daunted Mona and me as we set off for the town to purchase one or two necessities. I found five five-piastre pieces from my Alexandria days, very black with time, but for all that, still representing 25 piastres (3/-). I was determined to use them and thereupon shone them up beautifully – as I thought – with some Goddards of great reputation. I produced them – feigning the utmost innocence in the shop, as due payment for some wool. But the Egyptian, who was, it must be presumed, a rogue and a villain, flung them back at me with robust scorn and asked me, 'Madam, what are these?' I feigned surprise (I hope) and hurt that my money could be questioned. After all, it was good money, if only recently polished, but remembering that Egypt suspects the money she mints and circulates herself, I accepted defeat and withdrew. But not I fear without telling the gentleman what I thought about him and his countrymen. Prices had soared out of all proportion since we had left: one price for Egyptians and quite another price for the British is their age-old policy and they seem to get away with it. I must add that the next shop took my money without question, so my labours were not unrewarded.

Shopping finished we were wending our way to the nearest hotel for a drink, before returning to the ship, when apropos nothing, Mona said, 'There is Ken!' I hadn't seen him but there, sure enough, after eleven long months he was in the army lorry and yelling at his bewildered driver to stop and, jamming on the handbrake himself, he literally leapt out and dashed across to us. It seems he had heard of our coming and was even then on his way to the ship. We had a drink at the French club at Port Tewfik and then went back to the ship where we talked and we talked and we talked.

I learned for the first time that the poor soul had been torpedoed on the way back from Cyprus, jumping into the sea with his cine camera clutched tightly in one hand, later to be picked up by a small boat and then a large one and landed eventually in Alexandria and that later, in Libya, his lorry was twice bombed and he twice got severe concussion which meant a field hospital for a fortnight each time. All this and I knew nothing of it, because he didn't think it necessary to worry me. I felt much shaken by it all. He told me that he had written at least twice a week, and had sent me four cables recently, four blouses from Cairo and a camera compact with duty prepaid. Neither the blouses nor the camera had arrived and probably only fifty percent of his letters and he was most disgusted about it all. He was thinner and very nervy and excitable and I felt so sorry for him. He hopes to go on leave to Jerusalem complete with cine camera, in a few weeks. He thought too that he should be going to Tobruk in charge of a petroleum factory there. That was to have been in a month or two but today comes news that Tobruk has fallen: a black day indeed and almost incredible news after so long a siege. So Tobruk is 'off', which is just as well for Ken, I feel; it has always been an undesirable spot and one hates to think of anyone one knows being sent there. Well he won't go now – perhaps he'll be sent back to India, as that also, it seems, is on the cards.

Ken went about 10.30pm – back to Geneifa, 38 miles away. He was on the wharf again next morning however, before breakfast, and I had to send him away because the ship was moving to another berth and we were embarking patients that morning. He came back again after lunch and left again when we did about 3.30pm. He was so delighted, poor lamb, to see me again and hated to see us on our way. He spoke of being married soon, but I persuaded him that it was better to wait till after the war. I went to bed after that, being on night duty, and here I am on the fourth night of the trip out from Suez at 3.30 o'the morning. We have only seven BORs in B Ward, all up, and one British officer and one Sikh captain in A Ward. C Ward is completely full of Indians again.

And Mona – as I was – is entirely happy with them. There are three epileptics who 'fit' fairly regularly and one of the poorer mental cases went madder than normal and decided to attack one of his fellow sufferers today, while he was busy having a fit, so it was thought wiser to remove him to a padded cell. Another mental case has the disarming habit of ever wrapping about four blankets around himself and several towels around, turban wise, on top of his head, and then complaining in a loud voice that he is hot. Well, considering we are in the Red Sea and that the rest of us are simply dripping with heat and ennui, it may be supposed that he must be – hot!

Port Sudan – this morning early

It's the same flat, hot dusty place that it was nearly six years ago when I sailed back from Australia to Wales … We embarked a few patients from here, but left about 11 am and are now making for Massawa which, it is said, we should reach tomorrow afternoon. Yes today is depressing enough with its news of Tobruk and the ominous parlous condition of Sebastopol.[53] Who can see the end of it all – where and when?

The wireless is an enormous encouragement to keep awake. Without it I would not have had the courage to carry this record on, and up to date. We should be back – either in Karachi or Bombay – in twelve days so there should be nearly seven weeks' mail. Lovely! That's if it hasn't been sent to Cape Town or Timbuktu. Not much news of Port Moresby these days.

One wonders what the Japanese are playing at – Australia, India – perhaps Siberia as they have now occupied an island in the Aleutians.[54] Time will tell. Clwyd is, of course, in the forces in Papua – an incredible thought – and Glyn in a camp somewhere or other. Mona is presumably in the same spot and I'm on the high seas. Father has sciatica and Mother's dermatitis had returned to her upper hand. What a depressing miserable business it must be for her and now all this worry about all of us.

Of course, we are all right here except that we are completely tired of the ship and its personnel. We were subject in Karachi to some particularly petty restrictions regarding portholes but a spanner borrowed from the engineers did the trick and so we do not sleep with our portholes closed for all their orders. One day I'd like to tell the captain and the chief (jitterbug one, two or three) and the CO, British Army Incorporated, exactly what I think of them. I hope the opportunity occurs but I doubt it as they have long been afraid of us and endeavour to escape from us when we inadvertently meet on deck. We have had a lot of irritation from certain quarters and considerable amusement as well. It's a great life! As I write this there is a service from St Martin's-in-the-Fields on the wireless; so near and so far, but apparently things go on much the same in England, even in these days.

June 24th 1942

We sailed into the Massawa in the early afternoon the day before yesterday. I got up about 5pm and from my porthole I could see facing the deck handsome, typically Italian, buildings of the Promenade D'Italia. The whole waterfront was rather more interesting than most ports of call. The handsome villa-cum-palace of the late Duke of Aosta rose white among green palms on the water's edge. Wright and I were walking on the decks, seeing what we could see, when a car pulled up below and the docks' officer, who had just left the ship, asked if we would like a lift into town. Of course, we said thank you very much but we aren't allowed ashore. After a few minutes reviewing the situation, I was persuaded to step into the car, cap and all – shore leave or no shore leave – and off we went (Mary was on duty, so returned).

We went first to enjoy a *caffé frappé* in the best Italian tradition, in the Lido, an open air café with a swimming bath attached, rather dusty and faded, but adequate. Then we skirted the town, such as it is. The native population is Negro and Arab, fairly mixed. The women wear a garment derived from the sari – less glorified. The Italian population apparently still roams about at large, only more or less under supervision. It seems there is an army of occupation which administrates justice according to Italian ideas. It sounds a trifle odd but maybe it's alright. The docks officer turned out to be a South African from Durban and he and a naval officer and two pilots (one a tough looking ex-sheep station manager from Queensland) came on board for a chat.

But the chief remembrance of Massawa for all of us will simply be the heat. It seems there are degrees of heat, even of extreme heat, and that was the superlative of them all. No one slept on the ship last night as we were still alongside. The poor patients, disgracefully overcrowded, simply queued up for air under the few fans which were available. Others were lying in heaps on the decks, which are strictly taboo, but I hadn't the heart to send them down. It would do British Army Incorporated the world of good to spend one whole night in C Ward for a change just to see how they would enjoy it. It is a sheer disgrace. I was called to supervise two epileptic fits and I felt it would be a good thing if I had had one myself. At least I would ensure complete oblivion for at least five minutes and that would have been better than nothing. We drink and drink – gallons – and then we drip and drip until our skins are sore with mopping. No-one talks of anything else but the heat; it is all absorbing. Even Tobruk seems far away and long ago and of little significance compared with our immediate problems of how to get air and a breeze. But we left at dawn this morning and at least there is a breeze now. We reach Aden early on Thursday and then after that, to add to our troubles – monsoon seas. Well as long as it is cool, I don't care personally if the odd ship turns inside out. And why we didn't let Mussolini keep Eritrea, I can't think. Surely, no one in their senses *could* want to run the colony.

June 26th 1942

Aden is behind us two days since but until last night the seas were calm enough (sheltered it seems by Socotra island)[55] and it was still hot and extremely sticky. Last night we developed a graceful roll and today we are getting our teeth into it nicely. Good old monsoon, haze over the stormy sea, overcast skies, a cool wind (for which thanks be) and the whirr of the propeller as the aft-end of the ship rears itself out of the water. At breakfast we had to clutch our eggs in one hand and our coffee in the other to save them from disaster – and ourselves. The patients are lying around much as if their last hour had come. It's horrible for the poor things: even if they are not sick now they will be by tonight, at the sight and sound of everyone around them. I sat out on deck between 2 and 4am with my feet on the rails and drifted pleasantly into a semi-comatose state, where I felt nothing.

The news is frankly bad and somehow I can't feel particularly confident about Egypt. For one thing I believe that if we have too many reverses the Egyptians would have no compunction in going boldly over to the Axis. That would be jolly! And it seems we just haven't the up-to-date tanks and other equipment that the Germans are using. It seems to me, knowing nothing about military strategy of course, that if this was the real reason that we failed to keep Tobruk, it may well prove a like reason for failing elsewhere. It doesn't bear thinking about. The latest news is the Germans are 30 miles west of Mersa Matruh[56] and still advancing along the desert railway but drawing into the coast road. The general opinion is that a great battle for Egypt is imminent.

Four more nights for us if we are lucky enough to get in earlyish on Wednesday afternoon. It seems that a chit came through at Aden, this time for Poona, asking if our applications for transfer still held good. I should say they do indeed! Words to that effect will be sent to Poona as soon as we reach Karachi, I expect, and it may be that our transfers will eventuate fairly soon. Anywhere, oh anywhere at all, to get off this ship although it has been a relief to have the place to one's self at night. I think I should have gone into a nunnery at an early age. Most people annoy me if I see too much of them but there are the chosen few of course and I'm sure they'll be duly flattered if they knew. No doubt there is something radically wrong with me; the entire universe can't all be queer.

June 30th 1942

Mersa Matruh has been evacuated and some prisoners taken – the Germans claim 6,000. The position at the moment is again obscure. One hopes that something will happen to stop the rot but I fear that Egypt will fall. The Egyptians themselves will be no help at all – we can count on that. The Russian front has begun again in deadly earnest and although Sebastopol still holds on, the whole position could scarcely be grimmer. We all feel rather depressed and dumbfounded but no doubt the gloom will move off after a time and we shall still go on. Karachi tomorrow and thank heaven for that. I positively look forward to seeing the place again, although I'd never have thought it at one time.

The Parry family at the Manse Penshurst, Australia, 1912.

QAs on board troopship *Otranto*, 1940.

Being entertained in Cairo, 1941. Bimbashi is 3rd left.

(Left to Right) Mona Stewart, Bill Williams and Joyce Parry.

Camels through the desert, Egypt.

Joyce in 1941.

Patients in a ward in Alexandria.

Joyce with Italian POW patients.

Mona Stewart and Joyce shopping in Alexandria.

QA nurses on board *Karapara*.

(Right to left) Joyce, Mary Wright and Mona Stewart on *Karapara*.

Ken Stanley (left) and friend in the desert.

Joyce and Bob in Basrah.

Joyce and Mona Stewart in mufti,
Majestic Hotel.

View from Joyce's room overlooking
lake, Loreto Hospital, Calcutta.

Joyce in India.

Taj Mahal, protected with scaffolding, 1943.

Train up to Darjeeling, 1943.

Joyce on her wedding day.

David Herbert Davies.

July 26th 1942

It is nearly a month since I wrote herein and most of what has happened is too unpleasant to record. We went to bed after the last night duty and left the day staff to carry on disembarking patients. About mid-day Mona came in with the mail, twenty or so letters, including several from Mother which, being lengthy, I always leave until last. There were several magazines and books from Mali including *Owain Glyndwr*,[57] a selection of modern verse by Anne Ridler,[58] Virginia Woolf's *To the Lighthouse* and two booklets about my beloved Wales. Dear Mali, how generous she is, and how I wish she wouldn't do it.

There was great excitement too when the ADMS arrived and announced that four transfers had come through. Matron was definitely posted to Calcutta but she foolishly didn't find out about the remaining three. However, we naturally surmised that they were for us and, when next morning we set off for Bombay for repairs, we faced the monsoon more or less light heartedly, thinking it would be our last trip. But when we did arrive we were horrified to hear that the transfers were for Isaacs, D'Silva and Gomes and there we were all packed up and nowhere to go except – 'down to the seas again'.[59] It was a real blow and it left us very flat and restless, more particularly as we sat out in mid-stream, awaiting orders to go to dock, daily, for about ten days. I took to my cabin one day and just didn't emerge at all. I felt I couldn't bear to see anyone. Matron did the same on another day. We'd all had quite enough of this ship's atmosphere and were very nervy and fed up. To make things worse we had to turn out of our cabins and sleep in B Ward – like a lot of schoolgirls – and there was simply nowhere to go where we could get away from it all.

Worst of all, the CO informed us that Mona and I were wanted by the censor at the STO's office. We were all assembled one morning and told that 'someone' had been found using a code and that henceforth all our letters had to be left open to be cleared by the ship. I know I had never sent any code by letter but I had sent some names in a letter which Captain Blanche delivered along with a watch to Mother, when he was called home. I couldn't remember whether I had been indiscreet enough to mention something pertaining to it; I didn't think it possible, but of course, I was, by this time in a state when I imagined all kinds of things. I was a little relieved, although sorry for poor Mona, when the CO told her that it was in one of her letters (sent back from Australia) that a code was discovered. He also murmured something about too much criticism of authority and administration. Well there would be plenty of that of course, but what business it is of the censor's we couldn't quite see.

We did get ashore eventually and were put up at the Women's Services Club along Marine Drive for five days. I got through the customs with my radio and David and his brother and two other Indians spent a lot of time repairing it and wouldn't accept anything for doing it at all. It is going well now, or it would if everyone shut down their fans but they won't do that until about next January, I suppose. Anyway, it'll be a great comfort to me in a mess, ashore. The interview with the senior technical officer proved less fearsome than we anticipated. Mine was simply in connection with a cable addressed to Bob in Karachi but Mona's was certainly more serious but she explained that she'd never used the code and made a suitable statement and we all parted friends. He did say however that the reason that some of us were not getting airmail was because they were simply destroying them when they had an irregular address. It seemed very high-handed to me but, as I was more or less culpable at the moment, I didn't say any more. Now that he has said so much, he is trying to deny the statement, realising I suppose that there might be trouble for someone if the matter was really investigated. Well, it is all behind us now and great is the relief thereof.

We went to a cinema every night that we were in Bombay, just for something to do. Then at the last moment, as it were, Mary's transfer came through – to Colaba, which was just what she wanted as Kevin hopes to get a shore job soon.

There are five new staff, Miss Day, Miss Frith, Miss Easterbrook and Miss Milne (acting matron) and at the last moment, to replace Mary, they sent Miss O'Connor – a regular of some years' standing who is really senior to Miss Milne. So we set off with two matrons all because of some glorious mess-up at headquarters. Miss O'Connor was soon out of the running with dysentery. The first three days were beastly, a nasty curl on the waves which affected almost everyone one way or another. I got off with a dull headache but Mona was rather seasick for a day or two. Then that ceased and we rolled into the Gulf. That was worse; it was about as bad as Massawa. We poured and poured all day and all night and we all felt much washed out as a result.

But we arrived yesterday, and are moored off the RAF jetty mid-stream. Danny came aboard about 7.30pm and later attacked the CO about our not going ashore. And what is more miraculous, he granted it. We dashed down and changed and got ourselves nicely into the motor boat, which was waiting to take us ashore, when it absolutely refused to move. We must have sat there for an hour, and being more saturated than I've ever been in my life, we decided to go up and dry off under a fan. After a long time Danny succeeded in getting another launch across and we picked up the car and called for Bob and Kathleen. After a drink at the Port Trust Club we went on home, but didn't have long there as the launch was to pick us up again at midnight. It was good to be ashore in Basrah again and among friends. Today is mighty hot and we are not allowed ashore until 5pm. We embark patients at 5am tomorrow so it will be early rising for once!

We went alongside about 1pm and Bob sent a car around for Mona and me and we called at the office for him and went on to the Port Trust Club, where we met 'Captain Smithers with the wonderful eyes'! I had a feeling going back to the ship that it was probably the last time I would set foot in Arabia. Well, *Vale Araby* with all your heat and dust and dirt and evil smells. There'll be things that I shall remember when these are forgotten: the full moon rising over the date palms, the soft cool night air, and the broad swift flowing river with paths of golden moonlight shimmering in the black night. And other things to which one does not give words, words being unnecessary, I suppose.

Since Basrah it has been so hot and sticky that we literally ooze forth by day and by night. Through the night however, or towards morning, we left the intense heat and humidity behind and now we are rolling again – not a decent, clean sweeping roll either, rather nasty. Most of the staff are down, Nellie, of course, and Bill, and Miss Easterbrook. Mona makes hurried exits at intervals. I'm alright but sleepy and heavy. I went down to C Ward to help to serve the dinners: roast pork, large chunks of it and incredibly fatty – on a day like this! It was bad enough dishing it out but nothing would have persuaded me to eat it. We get in tomorrow morning, thank heaven. I love my patients but I hate this weather. The thought that I have to strengthen myself for yet another voyage nearly drives me frantic but Miss Milne comforts us with the assurance that our transfers will be awaiting. So roll on Karachi!

August 12th 1942

Bombay

We arrived after a four-day trip – very fast for this old tub (she'd been de-barnacled in the dry dock in Bombay).

We went ashore that evening, Saturday, having heard that *How Green Was My Valley* was on at the theatre. We took a taxi into town to make sure of a seat, but alas it had finished the previous night after a two-week run. I could have sat down on the road and wept. We seem fated to miss it for some reason and just to make things jollier we found that we could not get in at any of the cinemas as they were all booked out. The town was seething with Americans and there was barely room to walk on the road, so we did a little shopping and retired to the Grand café for coffee and sandwiches and gharry'd home.

We went over to see Mrs McGlashan next morning to arrange about mail and our shoes which have been gallivanting between Karachi and Bombay for months and we haven't caught up with them yet. We went across again, taking Miss Milne with us to church and then to supper. It was arranged that we went over to tea on Wednesday which we did and we stayed for dinner; they are most kind to us always. They are simply unaffected and homely and we like them a lot.

Very little mail – two from Mother, one from Mona, two from Ken, one from Bob readdressed from Lloyds and another followed later. There is still another – much awaited – which remains elusive.

On Thursday we had sailing orders for Bombay. We knew we were going off soon but thought it would be ME. Well, it wasn't. We took the BORs for the BGH, Karachi, and brought them down here to Colaba. They were all up and about and scatty and I did duty on alternate days which was not arduous. We are still here well out in the harbour, almost at Blipbanta, and it's difficult to get ashore at all. Actually there has been no shore leave until today. Gandhi and Pundit Nehru and the leaders of the Congress party have been arrested and of course the expected riots have broken out. It would be unwise to go out after dark in any case, I suppose, as there has been a lot of shooting after dark but it is alright in the day. Anyway, it's terribly dull on board stuck here, miles from anywhere and I want to go to the dentist while I am here.

There is some talk that we may go into dock for some days, while they fix up the air conditioning, once again. If so I suppose we shall be sent to the Services Club, which may give us time for our transfers to come through. There has been the usual muddle and Miss Wilkinson has informed Miss Milne that she is doing her best to arrange for our transfer back to the Middle East. Bless the woman. She only wants to please us, I suppose, but it's all the CO's fault as he should have mentioned in our second application that we did not want to return there. He knew so much but, as usual, proved himself to be wrong. Colonel Fitzgerald has been transferred – would that he had been twelve months ago. Major Ramchandani takes his place as CO: he is kind and amiable and human but I fear it is an unwise step to have given us an Indian CO. He hasn't the standing or weight behind him – notwithstanding his goodwill towards us – and we fear the bridge, notably the chief officer, will over-ride him. Still he'll be much better about shore leave than the late CO and the feeling that the 'CO is aboard' has completely gone. Miss Milne is a delightful little soul: most human and business like. She has just come in now with a letter from Miss Wilkinson to say she has sent out orders concerning Mona and me and that if ME doesn't intervene in the meantime, we shall be taken off here and now, or so we hope. If I could be certain that our next trip was to Basrah and not to Suez I should prefer to remain for yet another trip despite the heat and seas. I am loath, really loath for each trip to be 'really for the last time' when I don't know how long it is all going to be. Yet I know for my own peace of mind and sanity, I must get off this ship.

The Germans are at the foothills of the Caucasus. It seems so awful to think that so far we have not been able to divert them to help Russia at all. In fact it seems rather bad all round. We have taken the offensive in the Solomons it seems but there is a lot of talk about delicate situations and confusion and so on, so it doesn't look entirely promising. The situation in Egypt remains static at the moment.

I have just had a letter from Mona and two from General. Mona says Clwyd followed up his malaria and dengue with dysentery. Poor old Clwyd; he can't have much resistance left after that dose; it's too bad. I've a fellow feeling for him regarding the dysentery as my tummy has been behaving badly for about a week. I've retired to my cabin yesterday and today, there being nothing better to do as I've been on fluids only. Mona has had measles, poor child, and Glyn is only about 40 miles down the line from where she is. So they are creeping further and further away from home. It's all rather sad.

August 20th 1942

Women's Services' Club, Bombay

We went alongside on the 13th and orders came on that morning about our transfers. Mona goes to Dehra Dun and I to Calcutta. We came ashore with the rest of the staff and have been staying at the club again. Our relief arrived that day – one called Barr – and that looks hopeful, but as the days whiz by it seems less so, as no-one else is appearing to take our places. On the 18th the rest of the staff embarked again – they were told they were sailing for Suez next day – so I determined to get myself off somehow or other and Mona and I set off to see the CO as soon as we knew. We reckoned that as we had been one short on the last trip and no-one noticed the difference, they could sail one short again. After some persuasion I was permitted to disembark and got all my stuff off that night. Mona came ashore to dinner here, and we went to the cinema afterwards.

I went to see Embarkation yesterday and they arranged my seat on the train for tonight 5.40. Whilst I was there I saw the captain who told me that their plans had changed and they were back on 36 hours' notice, instead of four. So there still remains a chance that another relief may come and Mona will be able to set off too. Mona came ashore on the 4pm launch and stayed the night with me here. She will see me off on the train which will be some comfort. Embarkation gave me a chit on Lloyds for Rs135, which is first-class fare (I pay second class on my concession) and the remainder is meant to cover excess baggage. I doubt if it will as it is so heavy. They used to be given one and a half fares, but recently it has been cut down. Our bad luck again! We are going into Lloyds this morning to finalise arrangements for mail and transferring our accounts. Then there are just the remains of the packing and I shall be off.

8.30pm Ichapur

We have stopped for dinner at quite a large station and I still don't know the name (all names removed, of course) but the guard said something that sounded like Ichapur. Outside are dozens of Tommies, tin hats an' all, whiling away the time singing mostly Scotch songs, though two at least insist on the occasional Irish air. Those who aren't singing are whistling and the rest are laughing and joking with the peanut wallahs. It's a cheery scene in the half-lit station and we might be anywhere in Britain. The bell has just clanged and thereupon it raised loud cheers from the troops, apropos of nothing, as far as I can tell.

All these youngsters so far away from home. Their mothers could hardly picture them as they are now but they seem happy enough, despite the monsoon rain that drips upon them through the leaky station roof.

Mona came down to the train with me and it was nice having someone to see me off on my newest adventure.[60] We got down successfully to the station, without the taxi breaking down under the strain, and a poor miserable little body tackled the lot quite cheerfully and I eventually embarked. I've managed miraculously to wangle a whole compartment – I nearly wrote cabin! Actually, I did ask the waiter a moment ago if I could have my coffee in my cabin and he looked very shocked – too much sea going, I fear – for me. The compartment is about 12ft x 10ft and very comfortable with a bathroom and shower attached. There are two long side seats and two above which, if necessary, come down like upper berths and a sort of dressing table with mirror and cupboards and odd racks and pegs.

As I appear to be the only female travelling (first class anyway) I have the whole place to myself and have my entire luggage with me. The sergeant in the RTO place told me that this was alright if I could get it in, but hearing so much about having to pay excess for baggage, I feel uneasy about it. I sincerely hope I shall have a good sleep, if intermittent; we stopped several times through the night and no Indian station is exactly quiet even in the night, it seems.

August 21st 1942

As I am writing we have stopped at Nagpur where we will have breakfast at 10.30am. I got rather tired of writing so opened a packet of biscuits which Mona put in for me and cut into my melon, which I bought as paw paw, but it wasn't really ripe. I went upstairs however and drank a cup of coffee. Hearing such tales about things being stolen from compartments when they are left empty, I hesitated but everything seems perfectly all right. A sweeper comes along in most stations and will sweep the dust for an odd anna. Everything is very easy and comfortable: there are six large windows, with wires and shutters and all lock from the inside so one feels secure enough. Nothing very interesting so far, except endless paddy fields, springing green and lush and under water with the recent rains.

4pm

I have just had lunch at Gandhi – a smallish station but quite a good meal and nicely served – and I am on my way again now. There has been a mountain range to the right and left now for the past hour or so – I wish I knew my geography better. And last night, just before sundown we came through some rather lovely country, rugged hills, quite close to us, and the sunset behind them, smoky red and orange, was a lovely thing to see. For the rest so far it has been still quite flat, plenty of trees and shrubs and everything a fresh green as far as the eye can see: a welcome sight indeed. The earth is deep red and the winding country roads with their straw covered bullock wagons look pleasant and peaceful.

5pm

Tea at Raipur Junction. For something to do I've read the book *The Grasshoppers Come* by David Garnett and I've begun another pair of stockings for Bob. I have hopes of finishing another two pairs before the summer is fled from Basrah, but time will tell. The carriage gets so filthy despite the sweepers' efforts that I scarcely like to handle anything at all, let alone white wool.

Bilaspur 7.15pm

I ate some more unripe melon and a biscuit or two and drank some water, being too lazy to get out of my slippers and walk across for dinner. A girl has got in plus a dog, so I shall have company for tonight.

August 31st 1942

Calcutta 47th British General Hospital

The train arrived about 11am and I got myself plus my baggage to the RTO's office. As usual they hadn't received the wire from Embarkation and didn't know of my arrival, nor, consequently, did the BMH. However, an ambulance took me, miles it seemed, by devious ways and many native bazaars to the original BMH. There, after waiting for about an hour Miss Dexter, the matron, arrived and decided what to do with me. It seems the 47th comprises various sections in odd parts of town: the BMH (Surgical), the Loreto Convent (Medical), the Davidian Schools (Dysentery) and a place for skin and VD somewhere in the wilds … and there may be more, for all I know.

Anyway I was sent to Loreto, an old convent about three miles out of Chowringee itself: it is large and rather battered looking, but the grounds are spacious with lawns, a lily pond, plenty of trees and a statue of the Virgin Mary to watch over us!

We are in temporary quarters only, it seems, and are to move to permanent ones shortly. Now we are in cubicles – one each, thank heaven – and, although we sleep on camp beds, it is not that bad. We have a large writing table and two smaller ones and a chair. No drawers or wardrobes but it seems there will be such pieces of furniture as well as beds when we move.

I have acquired a mosquito net which I badly needed after a week's subjection to mosquitoes.

I went on duty next day in a ward of 60 beds – malaria, dengue fever, and jaundice. The wards are really very nice – airy and open and bright – but the equipment is nil and daily it pains me to work under such conditions for the patients' sake. No sterilizing drums, no instruments and no thermometers – as they appear to be taken daily and no one replaces them – and very little of anything indeed except gallons of quinine which I dish out thrice daily to numerous patients.

The off-duty is good; a half-day every other day and a 10–1 shift on the other day. Even so my feet are sore and I am utterly weary at 8pm. I don't go to dinner – I can't think of food in this heat really – although we are on rations – but no food tempts me these days. I'd much rather fall into my cold bath and be ready for bed. I get myself out of bed in the morning at 6.30 in order to get a bath in the only available bathroom. I hate washing piecemeal at a row of basins and I don't know what to do about it at all. The bearer brings tea at 6.45 and breakfast is at 7.30. Wards at 8am.

It's good to have someone who will put buttons on my overalls and clean my shoes – two things I detest – and the bearer brings tea at 4pm to our rooms as well. The dhobi [washerman] calls every few days and a dursie [tailor] very frequently so we are fairly self-contained. I went with him on my first half-day to buy sheets and such at the market, which is a very good one, although more expensive than Bombay. I acquired a very large valise from a small boy who carried my things for me all afternoon. I paid him the large sum of four annas for it. I went in again with Sharpe, a New Zealand girl, two days ago and we had tea at Firpo's and then went to see the film *The 49th Parallel* before taking a taxi home. One can get into town in a rickshaw for eight annas or by ambulance if there is one, and there usually is, daily at 4pm. Taxis are Rs2. We pay messing at the rate of Rs12 a day, which is less than if we were on rations, which is all to the good. Still no sign of any pay from Poona and of course the Melbourne contribution is still missing, and will be I imagine until the end of the year. So I suppose I go monthly to the field cashier at the 'Fort' in order to keep myself going.

But the real thing that is waiting as ever is MAIL. I've had two letters from Mona, who should be in Dehra Dun now (her nursing relief arrived in time fortunately) and one from Mrs Mcluhan, who tells me that three hours after we left Karachi for Bombay, a cable arrived for me from Bob. And then a letter later. She enclosed these with the shoes and had sent the parcel off – registered – that morning (18th). I received the letter on the 28th. Floods and recent riots have, it seems held up the trains. But daily, I await the arrival of that parcel and its contents. I can't think why I haven't heard from home either, as Lloyds have my present address. One of these days I suppose I shall have a bundle but how these days drag. Meanwhile … it has rained heavily yesterday and today and consequently it is cooler. Calcutta is intolerably humid and still hot and … very tiring I fear it will be. I am having a half-day off, and instead of my siesta after tiffin, I decided to bring this up to date.

September 2nd 1942

I think it was the evening of the day I last wrote herein that coming off duty, one of the girls knocked on my door and handed me a parcel. The SHOES. I think they are rather tight (but haven't so far worn them on duty) but enclosed therein and for which I have been waiting so long, the letter. By this time it has grown to 55 pages, the largest ever-written over the period 5/6/42–5/8/42. So now I don't feel so neglected or bereaved. No mail from Mother, however, since I arrived or from anyone else.

I went up to the BMH yesterday to meet Morrison who is on night duty at the Davidian Schools. We went to the market and I bought more underwear – which is quite an obsession with me – and then had tea. Walking up Chowringhee later, I saw O'Connor who is taking Miss Tyndall's place in Assam, at an IGH and had coffee with her while she had dinner at the Grand and then took a taxi home, by devious routes, according to the sunshine or the taxi meter. Things started off badly at the hospital this morning. The bearer offered me porridge (ugh!) at least four times, then toast which is too thick and flabby to eat anyway and I rejected both. He then brought me kidneys on toast, which is poison to me at all times. In desperation I called for toast after about ten minutes, during which time I lost any desire to eat it so when he brought it I said, 'No thank you'. During the next five minutes it was brought to me at least three times and in desperation I got up and left breakfast-less. I think I shan't bother to attend again.

It is still raining in earnest but it is cooler and that means everything. I filled in another four forms for Miss Warner this morning. This is about my forty-fourth since I arrived here. Somebody must be interested in my life's history, I presume. And yet we are told – a shortage of paper. Oh! The army!

September 9th 1942

It is over two weeks since I arrived here and already I feel quite settled. Strange how soon one becomes accustomed to a new mode of life and new surroundings in these days. I like the ward and the girls and, as far as I can be in the circumstances,

I am happy enough. Letters are slow to arrive – except for the ones from Mona and Mary and the one from Bob. But I should mention – just by the way, so unimportant it seems nowadays, amazingly enough – that Poona has been moved to pay into my account Rs822, and again today a further Rs234 for travelling allowances. Now, of course, I feel extremely vulgarly wealthy and I had the urge to go out yesterday and spend some of it and for no good reason. I bought myself a dinner frock just to reassure myself that I had the wherewithal to pay for it, I think. It cost me just 100 chips and I feel grossly extravagant but entirely pleased and satisfied.

Pozner, the young MO of our ward (who is a poet of some worth) and with whom I went to dinner and a cinema one evening recently, has been posted somewhere in the jungle, much to his annoyance. Several girls are being posted elsewhere from the BMH and a minister is going up there from here. This reduces our staff somewhat. Scott was sent on an ambulance train rather suddenly yesterday – to Lucknow. One is liable to fall in for such things, I believe. And as Plunckett has gone to the BMH today, Fairweather and I alone remain in D3. As I write deep rumbles of thunder rend the air and the rain is descending in earnest. Some climate this!

September 20th 1942

I've been off with dengue: my first bout of real sickness since I joined the army. I felt rather queer one evening almost a fortnight ago, but thinking that nothing ever happens to me, I had my bath and very rapidly got myself into bed. Next day I realised that I really wasn't feeling very good but staggered around for two and a half days thinking I'd be alright and then gave in. There were two days when I wouldn't have cared what happened, I ached so abominably, and then I distinguished myself by fainting one bright evening – a thing I didn't think I was capable of, and that shook the household a bit. I felt so strange that evening, neither here nor there, and I remember noticing how everything went gradually dark and then oblivion embraced me. A lovely feeling it was – and I hated coming round. But now I am up and about but still feeling incredibly weak but picking up daily. I lost some weight and am drained of colour and I'm on a vile tonic, which should by the law of compensation restore my lost vigour.

I went into town yesterday morning to Lloyds to fix up my account and to pay in the mysterious cheque which arrived one day last week. I didn't know where it had come from, £7/6/-. It was telegraphed through the Commonwealth Bank of Australia, Brisbane, where I know no-one. Does someone think I am in financial distress, I wonder? The bank proposed the idea that someone has left me a legacy. It is all very mysterious but possibly, one day, I may hear more of it. Lloyds were exceedingly helpful and as I was feeling childishly weak and helpless, I was very grateful. I proceeded then to have my hair washed and then went on to see *Dangerous Moonlight*. Lovely music and then I came back and wrote to Bob. I have written to Ken, rather incoherently I fear. I feel very low about it all but it had to be done so – *Vale* Kenneth! Another chapter closed and another begun – as it began a long time ago when the world was young. Somewhere I lost the way but have found it again before it was too late. I had a mere 28 pages from Bob one evening last week. How long my letters seem to take to get through and I write so often too.

The Japs are only 35 miles from Port Moresby. I suppose poor Mother is feeling frantic about Clwyd. Maybe they'll try to get the 'pay' people back to the mainland. I hope – selfishly – that they do. I'd feel so much happier if we were off that island.

October 27th 1942

We have been in the new house now,[61] some time since and nice it is to be able to unpack and spread oneself into drawers and cupboards. I have a room with a view and a balcony overlooking the lake. It's delightful here early morning and late afternoons with the long shadows of the trees reflected in the lake. There are three tall palms etched against the sky in the far side of the grounds, like three sentinels. I look for them daily.

Mona is due on leave from Dehra Dun. She spent the first few days in the Great Eastern Hotel but didn't like it much, so moved in here for Rs3 per day. It's pleasant here and she can come and go as she wishes. It's good to see her again and to be able to go over old times and old friends – places and people that mean nothing to anyone here. She left for Darjeeling last Friday but returns on Thursday in time for my birthday, which is presumably Sunday. Thirty-four indeed – how aged I am becoming!

I am tired these days and my brain is weary with running or trying to run the ward with 54 patients and one orderly to help me. I hadn't one at all between 1pm and 8pm yesterday and just had to manage with the help of patients. I get through it all somehow: beds, temperatures, odd dressings, medicines, endless quinines – because malaria is an epidemic these days – meals and all the paper work which takes up so much time, but it doesn't please me to know that as far as the patients are concerned they don't get the personal attention which they should.

I hear from home occasionally, but I certainly do not get all the mail that is sent. Sister Mona is in the AIF now, somewhere in the north of Queensland. I sent off their parcel yesterday, held up because I was waiting for father's pyjamas from the dursie. I gave him 15 chips to get the material and it appears that after about a month's absence he had decided to clear off with the money. I bought a rather pretty bedspread recently and after carrying it around all yesterday afternoon and evening left it in the taxi at the mess gate. So it was goodbye to that. The next day I left two frocks at a stall in the market but they kept them for me, fortunately. The day after I did the same thing with a parcel which I left at the station, but someone discovered it just as I was leaving and chased after me with it. I think all this lapse of memory off duty is the reaction to coming off the ward when I really have so much on my mind. I'll be glad to be going on leave for more reasons than one: to get right away from every-one in the army will be a tonic in itself. I'm having my mosquito net put up again today – I was kept awake all last night with the brutes and, in any case, I don't want malaria.

Bob's letters come rarely now as he prefers to send an accu-mulation by ship as far as Karachi or Bombay. They are more than welcome when they do arrive but I have to wait so long in between. I am joining the Saturday Club as I go there occa-sionally, and as Mona is returning, it is a rather nice place to take her for tea: quiet and comfortable and nicer altogether than a café or Firpo's.

I bought some velvet for a dinner frock last week – cerise – and paid much more than I should for it. Still, I've wanted one for long enough and it'll be useful for leave as it will be cold then. Now I've got to find someone to make it up, I suppose.

November 15th 1942

Night duty, my fourth night on – and a battle of existence against mosquitoes. Mona went back last night before I came on night duty. I saw her into the Dehra Dun Express at 11pm. I was feeling about as low and spiritless as I've ever felt and although I was quite seriously ashamed of myself, I didn't seem able to pull myself together. I couldn't take in that she was going back and kept saying to myself that I ought to feel this moment more, that I might not see her again until after the war, perhaps not for years, if we are sent in different directions – who knows – but I soon forgot and began thinking again about how tired I was and how I wanted to crawl into bed and never get up again. I felt that I should have done so much more to make Mona's holiday brighter and more varied, but I couldn't think somehow and we just went to the cinema and dinner each half-day. She said she enjoyed herself but I rather doubt it. And now it's night duty, and my daily cares having dropped from me, I feel better already.

It's the endless stream of admissions and discharges and the paperwork that is involved that increases the strain. I think everyone is feeling it more or less. Four enormous tents have gone up in the hospital grounds and all patients go over there automatically when they start on pamaquin.[62] All this looks so well on paper and someone is bound to get the OBE out of it – maybe he thinks it's worth it; meanwhile the staff: the MOs, sisters and orderlies work themselves to a standstill and the patients hardly get a look in at all. I did join up originally as a nurse to attend the sick, but it seems I am nothing but a glorified office girl writing up papers all day long and I hardly ever get a chance to see a patient. It's a queer life.

Today a number of letters, nearly all Australian, but only one from Mother. I can't think what has happened to the rest. Nothing from Bob, except, while Mona was here and on the eve of my birthday, a cable in which was written: 'Will explain next airmail. Hope well.'

It intrigued us greatly at the time. Mona went to bed and got up trying to get to the bottom of it, for days. I've given it all up. There has been no airmail following it and nothing previous to explain. It was most disconcerting not to be able to understand the gist of it but I expect I shall know what it means one day.

I sat up until 4pm today and went to the Saturday Club for tea, but I am tired now and it's rather early to be feeling sleepy at 9pm. The wards these nights are seas of mosquito nets – every bed having its own. And really it's impossible to see who is in the bed and whether they are alive or dead. So one leaves it to the common sense of the patients within to call out in a loud voice if they want anything. There are a lot of sick boys in the hospital just now – mostly malarias, but more recently a number with enteritis. No one turns a hair nowadays if we have malarias with temps of more than 105; it's much more exciting to get in someone who isn't malaria for a change, say perhaps simple rheumatism or nephritis. One never hears of such a thing hereabouts – they appear to be rarities. Well, pre-serve me from having malaria anyway. So many of the boys who have come down from Assam have had relapse after relapse. Awfully depressing for them.

November 21st 1942

I am writing this in the lounge under a dim religious light before dinner and prior to going on night duty. I got up at 4pm today and went into town to have my hair done. I shall suffer for it tonight I expect. I have done about half my time I think and in a way I am sorry – there is much to be said for the night watches after all – peace and seclusion and a certain freedom of movement. It's a very social night duty this one. We begin to drink tea at 10pm, when one or another begins to drift across to my duty room. O'Sullivan from upstairs and 'Old Mother Brown' as she is known within the unit and usu-ally the OMO on duty, and perhaps others. This session lasts until 1am, possibly later, and then I proceed to get the supper ready for ourselves in D1. I trail hazardously downstairs with a tray full of dishes, praying all the way down that I won't drop them. Supper is a tedious and lengthy affair – usually we don't eat anything that is sent to us and I scramble eggs or some such thing. As Watson comes down for a decent supper, I find my time in D1 is prolonged. Sullivan goes across to relieve Watson and Brown is too busy to stay.

After the washing up, which I loathe at a dirty sink, and more often than not with cold water, a most depressing business, we go our several ways, do rounds, take a short walk by the lakeside and install ourselves once again until 4am. This is the signal for more tea – incredible although it seems written down in black and white – and everyone collects again, with the exception of the OMO who, it is to be presumed, is now well away in bed, and at 5am we really begin the night's labours. It is one hectic rush from then on. I wash the sickest patients for Jameson in C1, five of them, and by the time I do a morning round in each of the three wards and collect the temperatures and write the reports, it is 8 o'clock and with that – the day staff.

The moon is almost full and the last few nights have been perfectly lovely. The lawn has been pure silver and the lake is full of stars. There is silence and peace abroad instead of incessant chattering and noise of the day – a lovely feeling – and the night air is cool and soft and healing. No letters at all. I'm becoming resigned, I think. I just refuse to think about them at all. I've had two letters from Mona, however. She had her two days in Benares and found it full of local colour and not at all disappointing. She sent me a piece of lovely gold and cerise brocade, enough for shoes or a bag, and I am making an evening handbag out of it, possibly two. She watched them weave this actual piece – the threads are pure silver dipped in gold. She says the carving is very fine there and there are numerous interesting temples and of course the river – where the faithful bathe. She is back in Dehra Dun now, her train being only 24 hours late on arrival. She also is on night duty and has five tents to supervise.

I bought a very pretty little afternoon frock at Dora Smith's yesterday and it was a nice change to be able to buy something ready to wear instead of eternally having one made. The red velvet frock had to go back to have the neck altered slightly, which didn't please me altogether. Otherwise I like it immensely, although apart from being able to wear it on leave, if I ever get any in the hills, it will probably be useless.

December 4th 1942

Off night duty and after two days to myself, I go on D11 at 1pm today. Lovely to have two days all to myself. It reminds me of Colwyn Bay – coming off a case, saying nothing to anyone that I was free, doing what I pleased, suddenly making up my mind to spend the whole day walking through the woods and away beyond, within the sight of the hills. That was always enough – I could then return to my little room content. But there are no hills here, or anywhere to walk at all, save up and down the crowded city pavements, with their odd assortment of humanity – the khaki clad to the poor misshapen beggar. So I spend my free time in the market or in the more dignified city shops, buying things I don't need at all – filling in time.

Such a lovely morning, as I sit here writing, my windows open to the lake – full of blurred reflections, a light breeze blowing. Coolies pad up and down, barefoot, on the path below carrying stones, and from a distance the sounds of stones being cut. At times a white-clad sister walks across from the wards, dazzling in the strong sunlight: rather nice, it gives one a sense of pleasure, if only momentarily. The huts across the lake look already native in the grounds, and being brown, they look as though they had come up out of the earth, like mushrooms. I always, on my nightly rounds, thought them so cosy, the green turf on the floor, the long rows of beds with their scarlet blankets, the mosquito nets up, and the hurricane lamps hung up on the centre poles and the boys idly chatting in groups or sound asleep under their nets. And always their cheerful 'Good night, Sister,' as I stooped on my way out of the door and went out into the darkness and left them to their youthful schemes and dreams.

Mary sent me a copy of Walt Whitman's *Leaves of Grass* for my birthday with a nice cheerful red leather cover. And a calendar, a little premature but not so much, with a picture of Tagore on the cover and these lovely words: 'Let your life lightly dance on the edges of time; like dew on the tip of a leaf'. Well it would be nice, if one could manage it – somehow – but it isn't so easy.

Letters have been arriving at long last, including one from Father saying Mother is in hospital, having had an operation. And I didn't know. Well it can't be helped of course, but I always seem to be away on such occasions, when I might have been of help. I'm hoping that the enforced rest will cure her legs – it should, if anything does. There have been three or four from Bob too, explaining that at least two letters will not arrive. Rather a blow, after all the labour and time, and I could have done with them moreover. He hopes to get leave during January. So do I. Darjeeling perhaps, if it can be managed. How many months will that be, almost six, surely half a year? What a waste!

Two books from Mali and Phyllis. Steinbeck's latest *The Moon is Down* and *A Dialogue on Modern Poetry,* by Ruth Bailey, which should prove interesting. They are good to me. But I must now get into uniform and be ready for first lunch. I've been reading Virginia Woolf's last book, *Between the Acts*. I always liked her style – so fluid and light, merely touching the edge of things as though it were too painful to penetrate deeper. I can imagine that she might end up as she did, not knowing what to make of the unending tangle of her life. It is disturbing in a way too – one sees so much of one's self in her characters – their minds, their thoughts – trailing on and on, never getting anywhere.

December 14th 1942

A day off and such a lovely, lovely morning. How really perfect these days are in December here. I must go out and do some solid thinking and shopping for Xmas. My money is all in a glorious muddle again – the army has now decided to take out some advance of pay, which I drew in Cairo at the beginning of 1941! Well, I hope they know what they are about, for certainly I do not. Bob's letters are coming through in about eight days now, which is better. He still talks of leave in January and I've cabled to find out the approximate date of his arrival so that I can ask for leave at the proper time: I don't want to muddle things.

It's the mess dance on the 22nd and I believe the MOs are giving us a cocktail party on the 29th. So what with Xmas dinner and all the festivities in the wards, we'll be occupied enough.

What a terrific surprise two nights ago. I came over to the mess after duty at 8pm and found two Christmas cakes awaiting me. One from home, which Father had asked Mrs Clements to make as Mother is in hospital – and one from Deanie: lovely delicious home-made cakes. How we will enjoy them – here in a land where all cakes are bought. The trees that look like replicas of a Japanese watercolour are stirring lightly in the breeze, just disturbing the mirror-like surface of the lake. I shall miss this lovely outlook if I am ever transferred to the BMH and I have an awful feeling that perhaps I shall be when I return from leave.

I have a card from Gwen's husband Ronald saying, 'Ronald Gareth was born November 25th'. How thrilled they will be and I am so pleased for them. Gareth is such a lovely name.

December 20th 1942

Nothing much to report. The viceroy's lady – after four attempts – eventually paid us a visit a few mornings when I was alone as Harris had gone off in an ambulance train. The boys were very good and the ward looked rather nice although it probably shouldn't have. I had to curtsey and all that on being introduced and was told afterwards that I was 'observed' from the top balcony, which thankfully I was unaware of at the time, as I am sure I should have giggled or something equally monstrous.

Then Mary turned up – quite suddenly. She has been here about three days but left early this morning with Goodridge, of all people, and some others, plus several Indian VADs for Bamilla (district of Calcutta) to form part of a new IGH, the 92nd. It was nice to see her and she is just the same Mary.

The mess dance is the day after tomorrow and after that a cocktail party in the MOs' mess. Then Xmas before we recover from that. But all I really feel interested in is leave – which, I hope, will be soon.

Christmas Day 1942

Eleven o'clock and the end of the day, thank goodness. We decorated the wards as best we could with our 'newspaper funds' and D2 looked quite festive, with streamers and four long tables down the centre of the ward, and lots of flowers and leaves. The dinner was quite good too, with beer and cigarettes all round. Odd people drifted in and out all day, in the usual fashion. Tea followed almost on top of lunch and supper followed tea. When we left at 8pm, everyone looked completely overfed and ready to sleep. A terrible post-Christmas dinner depression always sets in, when it's all over and one is glad to escape. We thought of bed but for some reason or other the MOs' mess decided to ask us over for drinks and to dance there afterwards. As usual it was a complete washout and I have escaped up here to write some letters and this, unnoticed I hope, although I don't much care.

There was quite a raid last night – Christmas Eve – a bomb dropped on the city among the troops and 20 were seriously wounded and died. So last night the BMH was operating all night. There have been raids over Calcutta in the past five or six nights but last night was much the worst. This building shook with the vibration so it must have been very near. I suppose they'll continue while there is a moon, which is now full.

December 28th 1942

Off this morning: a perfect morning, cool and sunny, with birds chattering and the merest murmur among the leaves on the trees at the lakeside. I went for a walk yesterday morning – solitary – my first since I came to Calcutta, away, beyond and behind the hospital. Through numerous small native villages where the children popped out wide eyed to watch me pass: wattle and daub huts with straw-covered roofs by the roadside or among the palm groves; nursery gardens full of cosmos and marigolds strangely bright and fresh and clean to be springing out of the dust and dirt. One small boy came up to me and asked, 'What time is it please?' and I was delighted to be able to tell him it was quarter to three. He repeated it carefully and solemnly and thanked me and departed; quite a hero among his compeers I fancy. Then a young man stopped and asked me if I was looking for any particular house and I was sorry to have to tell him, 'No' and that I was 'just walking'. He said, 'Just walking' after me and I said, 'Yes, just walking' and we laughed together and went our ways. They were all sitting cross-legged in the sun on the roadside or on the grass under the palms. I envied them their careless uncomplicated days and the ease with which they walked barefoot while I, with two large blisters on my heels, laboured on my homeward way. It was pleasant to get away and it reminded me of my many solitary walks in *Cymru fy*, when I felt free and envied no one, swinging along some narrow country lane and within sight of my beloved hills. No hills here – as flat as your hand and dusty and dirty if you like to look at it that way, but it has some appeal and I shall remember India pleasantly enough when I am far away.

It is difficult to get taxis now, I believe, although I haven't been in town for a week or so. Firpo's was closed on Sunday night because they literally had nothing left to sell. And at the Grand, where amid the panic of the recent raids, all the bearers have left, I believe one has to line up with a knife and fork and spoon, like the troops, and forage for oneself in the kitchen.

Judi, my bearer, tells me that he is going 'after fifteen days' because his wife and child 'both cry' when the raids come. I am sorry he is going; he has looked after me so well. I never have to ask him to do anything – he just 'knows' beforehand. I don't blame him for going for I am sure there is little, if any, provision for their protection if things did get bad. I am sure they won't, but they don't know and why should they wait to see. After all they are perceived to be like children in the minds of the army officials and aren't expected to act differently!

I've just been lecturing some of the boys in the ward for talking nonsense about India and the Indians. To hear some of them talk one would imagine that they were the ones who were 'uneducated' and 'uncivilised' as they call the Indians. It causes such bad feeling and it's only lack of thought. One boy told me that there was no part of India which was worth looking at and he's been to Darjeeling and the Himalayas. Probably, he's never moved out of his home village before this war, and when he does go home, no doubt he'll complain bitterly about the English weather and how marvellous India was. How contrary human beings are – never, on principle, content with their little lot.

It's our Christmas dinner tonight but there is nothing exciting about that when you've dished up Christmas dinner for 65 patients a few days before. The novelty of duck and Christmas pudding has greatly worn off.

I am getting restless about my leave and I think if I hear nothing further before, I shall ask for it from about the 6th or 7th January. I am so afraid I shall be sent to some remote spot beforehand.

January 1943

Benares – Agra – Darjeeling – Calcutta
Bombay – ambulance trains

On leave. Benares. Agra. Clarke's Hotel

After tossing around various ideas about how to spend the first two weeks of my leave, I decided almost at the last minute to take the train for Agra,[63] and to break my journey at Benares.

I managed to get a single compartment all to myself and had a comfortable night after boarding the train at Howrah at 7.20pm (the Punjab Mail). Nothing very interesting en route but the country was pleasant enough with rice and mustard fields and scattered villages and odd towns. I arrived at Benares at around 4pm and got myself a room at Clarke's hotel. It was pleasant there in the cantonment, a long low whitewashed building with wide verandas overhung with bougainvilleas. The steps were a mass of chrysanthemums in pots and the garden colourful and gay. That afternoon I took a taxi and a guide and set off to see the sights. First the 'Mother India' Temple opened by Gandhi some years ago: not very interesting or beautiful. The floor was almost entirely taken up with a huge map of India in marble bas relief. Then, the town: just a succession of bazaars and stalls, straggling and dirty. The 'Golden Temple' in which every Hindu is supposed to worship once in his life is apparently very sacred but it is also very tawdry and dirty. Through a hole in the wall we saw the worshippers offering flower petals, leaves and holy water from the Ganges to the god Shiva. The floor was wet and slippery and I'm afraid I was more concerned about not sitting down on it, than able to give my mind to what I could see. Beyond was the temple of the sacred bull Nina but the whole place smelt so terribly that I touched as gracefully and rapidly as I decently could. I would think that they kept a whole herd of bulls and cows somewhere behind the scenes.

I bought some brass at the brass market where they had much that was fine and lovely. And next morning I went to see them weaving the lovely brocades. Children (paid five chips a month!) turned the large shuttles in and out as to the manner born. The brocade is sold in the shops for 30 chips a yard and sometimes much more. It all seemed wrong to think that those who did the actual work received so little. I bought a few pieces for shoes. The trip down the river was really pleasant and most interesting: Mother Ganges, where every Hindu must wash once in his life to become holy. Herein they wash their clothes, themselves and their brass pots; herein too they throw their dead infants (up to two years), the ashes of criminals and their own ashes. The river front is high and much built upon in terraces. Here the Maharajah of this and that builds his house and installs his relations or perhaps his superfluous wives. In between, rise the spires and domes and minarets of other days. The burning Ghats are on the river bank where the nearest relative sets the funeral pyre alight. The ashes are then consigned to Mother Ganges and go on to reach the sea, 'that gathers all things unto her'.

There was a very lovely garden not far from the hotel and I sat there in the warm sunshine on the last morning and re-read *The Prophet*:[64]

This day has ended.

It is closing upon us even as the water lily upon its own tomorrow.

What was given us here we shall keep

And if it suffices not, then again must we come together and together stretch our hands unto the giver.

Forget not that I shall come back to you.

A little while, and my longing shall gather dust and foam for another body.

A little while, a moment of rest upon the wind and another woman shall bear me.

Farewell to you and the youth I have spent with you.

It was but yesterday we met in a dream.

You have sung to me in my loneliness and I of your longings have built a tower in the sky.

But now our sleep has fled and our dream is over, and it is no longer dawn.

The noon tide is upon us and our half waking has turned to fuller day and we must part.

If in the twilight of memory we should meet once more, we shall speak again together and you shall sing to me a deeper song.

And if our hands should meet in another dream we shall build another tower in the sky.

There is so much that is beautiful and true in this philosophy and it is so little different from the truths of Christianity, after all is said and done.

I left Benares after lunch on Saturday and caught the Delhi Mail from Mogul Serai. There was one ladies' compartment (first) only and that a single one which was occupied, so I had to choose between the company of four British officers (first class) and two Indian women (second class). I chose the latter. One was a woman, poorly clad with silver bracelets on her ankles, who sat cross legged on the seat imperturbably. She had two enormous baskets of guavas but I didn't see her eat at all during the 14 hours that I was on the train. The other was a schoolteacher from a convent in Delhi; a bright intelligent young woman who spoke English perfectly, although with the usual intonation. She was very dark and very attractive. She told me she had a brother who was a medical student in Patna. She had taught in various parts of India and had also, for a time, been a governess to the children of some Rajah. She was a delightful companion.

All would have been well except that at Allahabad a Mohammedan lady and two young children got on with their luggage, rather with all their possessions, I think. I counted six large suitcases, two huge bedding rolls, a basket, a tiffin carrier, a large earthenware pot of water in a cumbersome wooden frame, another silver water carrier like a teapot, a portmanteau and sundry other odds and ends. It was a rare sight to see the floor. I was very cross because they peremptorily decided to pull down the old lady's baskets and proceeded to stack all their cases on the upper berth. I went out and produced the guard – because one is allowed only to take so much luggage into the carriage – the heavy stuff is supposed to go in the guard's van, but he was worse than useless. All the relations talked all at once, very loudly and rapidly and with appropriate gestures, and kissed their sister or wife or cousin, whatever she was to them, not once but many times and the grave-eyed children also and I, at length, retired and gave it up as finished.

We set off on our way again and the party on the floor proceeded to settle itself for the evening meal and after that to sleep. The tiffin carrier disclosed endless pieces of meat and chicken bones, which, with chapattis, they proceeded to eat with their fingers. After that there were sundry other things and a drink of water all round from the earthenware pot which satisfied the family. The mother then rummaged in the hold-all and produced two gaudily embroidered pillows, something that looked like a curtain, over which she spread a large mat, then several light eiderdown things and a woollen shawl or two. The children fidgeted and whined a bit but at last settled down to sleep. The mother reclined among the debris and refused my offer of the upper berth. She spoke English quite well and seemed a nice little soul unlike the rest of her relatives. She was most attentive to the children all through the long cold night. The little schoolmistress and I discoursed upon this and that; she had a lively tongue and I let her chatter on until we came to Cawnpore.

After that I tried to get some sleep, with my feet tucked under me in the corner of the seat. There was no room to unpack my valise and get out my blanket but oh how cold it was and how I longed for Tundi, where I was to change for Agra. I had been told by different guards at different stations that we would arrive at 6am, 2am, and 4am, 3am or 5am. All said helpfully that the train was two hours late but even that didn't cover the discrepancy in the time of arrival. But the Indian mind is philosophical and a few hours are neither here nor there and one is helpless against such an attitude and at length one accepts the situation and retires. I eventually got out at 5.25 after hanging out of every station en route and asking, 'Is this Tundi?' At Tundi I found a waiting room and the Ayah spread out my bedding roll for me on a couch and after some tea and toast I got down to it and slept until 7.30. We left about 8am and ambled into Agra cantonment at about 9.30.

There are positively no taxis in Agra so one uses a tonga everywhere and in that manner I arrived at Laurie's hotel. It looked a delightful place to stay but unfortunately there was no accommodation available and I had to go on to the Imperial. Only by luck did I get a room here – the occupant it appears is in hospital – and I am quite comfortable although it's nothing to rave about. There is hot and cold water however and baths are a treat to me, who in Calcutta, had to be content with two buckets of water at the bottom of the bath. I went to the Taj Mahal on the first afternoon. I was scarcely in the mood for it, being tired after the previous night, but the Taj would overcome all moods. One goes through a native area by car en route and then through the national park. The dome can be seen from afar, but it is now, alas, covered with scaffolding – some repairs taking place. But one forgets that at the first breathtaking sight, through the lovely arches of the gateway. What can one say of it that would not seem banal and prosaic? It is far lovelier than I dreamed of – most exquisite and most perfect in detail and in setting. I shan't begin to describe it as I shall see it in my mind's eye for all time: the nebulous pearl colour of its marble, the delicate lace-like screen, the flowers inlaid in the marble – jasmine, lily, rose, fuchsia or lotus – set in topaz, agate, jade, onyx and black marble collected from all over India; the graceful dome and arches, the exquisite carvings on the marble columns and walls, the tomb of Shah Jahan and his beloved queen – the Persian Princess Mumtaz Mahal; all these shall remain, as will the lovely garden, with its cypress trees and fountains and the reflections in the marble basin below. One could and should sit for hours and gaze upon the utmost perfection of it all, so full of peace it is – at one with past loves and glories, as with all time to come. Here in the garden are trees and shrubs from all over India: mango, paw paw, peepal (the holy tree), cypress, fir, eucalyptus, and silk oak, cactus, pittosporum and tamarind and others I know not. Cannas bloom riotously alongside hibiscus, poinsettias, syringa, jasmine, gaudy bougainvillea and many English flowers such as verbena, sweet peas and phlox as well as beds upon beds of roses and of course lilies, which are depicted among the mosaic work.

I went again next morning and Major Robertson, whom I met here, rooted me out while it was yet dark and we went again by tonga and stood above the lovely gateway and watched the first morning light rest upon the marble, bringing it to life and warmth again. So lovely it was in that first light with no one about at all and the dew still silver on the grass. A week later and I would have seen it by moonlight, when it is most lovely of all, but I shall miss that.

After breakfast I tonga'd again along the same route and to Akbar's fort of red sandstone with castellated walls, a moat and drawbridge; it covers a large area and the walls are a mile and a half in circumference. It was built early in 1500 and it must have been an amazing spectacle in its heyday, complete in itself with mosques and palaces and council chambers and bazaars. The guide told me that 10,000 people had lived therein. Here it was that poor old Shah Jahan was imprisoned for the last seven years of his life by his son Jehangi,[65] who was impatient for him to die. There in the lovely Jasmine Tower while the Jumna flowed below, he could see the Taj Mahal and the tomb of his dear Mumtaz Mahal, and there it was that he died an old man.

The Pearl Mosque is most exquisite, plain and dignified and unornamented except for the glorious carved archways and columns and the marble shines like mother of pearl, unspoilt, perhaps only more beautiful with time. Then the private audience chamber and the public one, where the king sat on his marble throne and addressed his subjects, and the palaces, one for his Hindu wife, and one for his Mohammedan wife. Then a sort of outdoor concert hall with a marble platform for the king and one opposite for the jester and below the walls alongside the Jumna, but still enclosed in the fort grounds, the arena, where wild beasts fought as they did in Rome – elephants and tigers and so on. The lovely Jasmine Tower, where the king died, looks over the river to the Taj. Here is another of those most exquisite marble screens. Whole windows are carved out of solid pieces of marble; the light filtering through on all sides gives the impression of delicate lace which lights up the semi-precious stones of the inlaid flowers in the walls. There is a bathroom with a marvellous roof studded literally with thousands of tiny mirrors and when it is lit up with magnesium wire, the whole effect is brilliant and bizarre. There are numerous other baths in the various courtyards with fountains playing – marble beautifully curved and carved – sometimes with seats around them. Apparently they were fond of bathing and in public under the blue sky. The guide told me that they had hot and cold water and that rain water was supplied from the roof. The special bath for the queen, where she washed her hands and face before eating, was always filled with fresh rose water. There are niches in the walls where fresh flowers were put every day. Then the floor of one courtyard was inlaid as a game – similar to ludo – and the king and queen and their court sat around and played with dice and called out the numbers. We were told that the pieces were children dressed in different coloured clothes.

During the mutiny of 1857 the fort was used as a hospital and 30,000 British were housed within but it was never besieged.

In the afternoon I went with Major Robertson to Dayalbagh a few miles out. Here a temple or memorial is slowly being raised to the founder of this comparatively new faith, Radha Soami. He is buried within. The major took me to see an old Dutchman who lived in the cottage of the grounds and who, after trying every religion once, has at last found peace in this one. The model of the memorial, which he showed us, is a most stupendous and amazing piece of work, or rather it suggests it will be when completed. Already the workmen have been working for 25 years or so and only the foundations and up to the first floor are completed. It is also of solid white marble with columns of 12 sides, most amazingly carved with fruit and leaves and flowers at their tops: great sunflowers and mangoes and creeping ivy and exotic lily – all the Indian flowers and fruits. There are slender columns between of pink and black and a lovely green marble, all from different parts of India. The founder's tomb is on the first floor of marble and inlaid like the tombs in the Taj with flowers and semi precious stones. The archway and ceilings are delicately carved and curved.

When it is complete it will comprise almost every type of architecture – Gothic, Norman, Doric, Moorish, Byzantine and Mogul. It sounds an awful hotchpotch but it is so immense and the work so amazing that I feel it will be worth seeing when completed – although I hardly think at the present rate of progress it will be in my day. It can never hope to have the infinite grace of the Taj; it is too heavy and too ornate but the marble itself can never be anything short of beautiful and I think it will succeed. Most of the workmen give their free time for love of the founder and here around the grounds they cut and saw and carve the huge blocks of marble that come from 150 miles away by oxen cart. So must the scene have been, at the building of Solomon's temple, the great cathedrals and mosques of antiquity; the same sounds of chipping and sawing, the same primitive tools and workmen with the same love of their ancient handicrafts. It was a solemn and immense thought – actually to watch the building of this future work of art, to walk on its walls and watch the huge corner stones and archways being slowly hauled up by human hands, for there is no sound of machinery and nothing to jar in the making of it all. There are the same inlaid flowers in precious stones set in marble as are found at the Taj, but there is more elaborate carving here around the massive pillars and altogether it will be more ornate.

There is an adjacent model village belonging to the same estate, where leather goods are made and cloth is woven and shoes are made, everything done by hand. I was so interested in it all and may have missed it so easily, for it is not generally spoken of or even known about, by the casual tourist.

Yesterday morning I went out to Akbar's Tomb – old Akbar the great Mogul emperor who united almost the whole of India in the 16th century while Elizabeth reigned in England. It is the same lovely red sandstone, wonderfully carved, and the four gateways are inlaid with coloured marble in intricate designs. Inside many of the gold paintings are worn away, or have been looted through the centuries, but the marble work remains as lovely as ever. Here Akbar is buried and many of his relations also. The grounds are spacious and beautiful and one should really spend the whole day here. There was no one else at all in that vast enclosure and it was sunny and clear and infinitely peaceful.

In the afternoon I went out to see Itimad-ud-Daulah's tomb, across the Jumna. It is a perfect little gem, similar to the Taj but much smaller. There are again the inlaid flowers in the marble. Almost the entire walls here are inlaid and the marble screens, which form the windows and the beautiful balustrade of marble around the roof, are more delicate and lovely than words can describe.

The ride there, by tonga, was something to remember, through many bazaars and villages. It must have taken us quite half an hour each way to cross the bridge that spans the river. What an amazing spectacle it was: such a conglomeration of human beings and animals and vehicles one could find nowhere on earth but in India. Tongas and oxen carts, many with painted horns and gay garlands of flowers or coloured beads round their necks; tiny donkeys, laden with panniers of stones or firewood or anything at all, picking their way on their incredibly dainty feet in and out of the medley; boys on bicycles; an odd motor car; army lorries; carts with cage-like tops drawn by skinny underfed horses; women in gay saris or, more usually here about, full gathered skirts and tight shawls; naked or half naked children. In fact every variety of Indian and animal passed with us, at length, at long length, over the Jumna Bridge.

On the roadside: all the vendors squatting easily in the sun: the local barber shaving his clients; the scissor grinder; the dursie cutting his cloth; women delousing each other's hair; dhobis and women washing in the river with their garments spread out to dry on any nearby fence or the bare ground itself; the oxen cart carrying great loads of stones or bricks or hides or bales of cloth – their brass bells clanging as they ambled along; dogs barking, children playing in the sun, women walking wearily along with great bundles of washing or fire wood on their heads – so gracefully they walk; old men with faces one would like to paint and young men with grave intelligent expressions. This is the real India rather than the India of the cities, more colourful, more varied and much more interesting.

And so I leave Agra this morning for Calcutta. It has been so full of pleasant lovely things and I wouldn't have missed it for the world. I should like to go to the Taj again this morning to say farewell, but there is no time. Perhaps one day I shall come back again – who knows – I hope I shall.

January 17th 1943

Calcutta

Major Robertson saw me off at Agra armed with a packet of cream crackers and a tin of gorgonzola cheese, together with some Christmas cake, chocolates and golden halva – an Indian dessert made of sugar, walnuts and ghee – which I find delicious having a depraved taste; he evidently didn't mean me to starve. The train obligingly stopped for quite twenty minutes quite near the Taj so that I could feast my eyes once again, before going on my way. I looked out of the carriage window until it was just a blur on the horizon and then I could see it no more. *Vale* Agra and so much that was beautiful!

Despite my booking a seat three days previously nothing had been done about it, as usual, and as the solitary 'ladies first' was occupied by two females, I got myself into an empty four-berth first compartment, only to be followed two seconds later by a Cingalese gentleman. He was as sorry as I was about it, but there was nothing that could be done, so the guard said. At Allahabad I spotted a major in the IMS on the platform so I went up to him and asked if I should go to bed as usual or what! He was highly amused and asked me if I would feel safer with him! Well of the two I think the Cingalese gentleman would have been the more reliable. However, he went along and spoke to the occupants of the 'ladies' and found that one was getting out at midnight so that I could transfer my things then, which I did, and all was well. As I was leaving two British officers arrived, so it would have been three to one; not that it matters in India, but it was much better for all concerned as things were. My travelling companions had lived in Burma for six years and had a small boy at school in Simla. They had lost everything of course in the Burma evacuation, having time only to bury their silver.

I had a good night's sleep and the day passed at length, rather wearily, and so we arrived at Calcutta at 7.25 and ON TIME. This was simply and solely because the Swami of Assam was on the train in a special white coach, and all along the way police with red pagris[66] guarded the stations. What awful deferential rot really in these days! I arrived at the hospital gates only to be told that the taxi must not go in because we were in quarantine – smallpox having broken out. We had been in quarantine before we left and we had all been vaccinated, but this fresh outbreak was new to me. However, it transpires that it wasn't as bad as it sounded, though there are some cases and some of the wards are definitely in quarantine. A lovely pile of letters to greet me including six from Mother from whom I hadn't heard for many weeks. It is reassuring to know she is well and strong again except for that awful dermatitis which still persists. A letter from Bob suggesting that I meet him at STO office in Bombay and a letter cable saying, 'Proceeding via Killarney. Wait my arrival!' It arrived on the 14th – re-addressed via the bank but in Calcutta on the 10th and according to the date, it left Basrah on the 9th – which doesn't seem possible when they normally take at least eight or nine days or longer. I reckon that if it left on the 10th or 11th, he might normally be expected to reach Karachi about the 14th–16th. The train journey I am not sure of, but it would take almost three days, I fancy. So all things being equal he should arrive on Tuesday, possibly even tomorrow. Sometimes when I re-read the cable I wonder if he meant me to go to Karachi and wait at the Killarney, although this didn't strike me at first. Even if I had done that next day (16th) I think I would have missed him, passing each other en route. I can only hope that everything will turn out without any unexpected hitches. As it is, I feel I daren't leave the mess in case a message comes through, or the gentleman himself arrives. It is almost six months since we were in Basrah – how hot it was and how far away and long ago. But now I wait.

February 10th 1943

On the morning of the 19th I had a telegram to say that Bob was arriving on the 20th. I had packed most things and was cleaning out drawers and generally tidying up when Deacon came up to say that Bob had arrived. It seems that he had sent a second telegram from Lahore, which I hadn't received, so unfortunately I wasn't at the station when he arrived. It was unbelievable that he had actually come and now, of course, he is gone again. We went into town at once to arrange accommodation for the night and got our tickets and reservations for the train for Darjeeling the following evening. There was an air raid that evening which cut short our dinner at the Grand but we went to the cinema later and saw a film, without further incident. We just caught the train the next evening with scarcely a minute to spare and settled ourselves for the night, arriving at Siliguri next morning at 6am and took breakfast at the station.

Then the long ascent up to Darjeeling with the great valleys below us, and mountains towering above us on either side. Tea plantations everywhere, on neat terraces, and luxurious tropical-cum-alpine vegetation: hibiscus, bougainvillea, poinsettias, ageratum, eucalyptus, tree ferns, acacias and all manner of other shrubs that I know not. We stopped occasionally at some funny little station, while the train took in water or coal or both. We wound in and around bends and puffed and climbed our way ever upwards the whole of the 7,000ft to Darjeeling. Since Siliguri the whole nature of the countryside has changed, and the people too – now distinctly Mongol in type – Tibetans. The women do all the chores and the men sit around smoking and generally enjoying life; the women carried everything on their backs, including their children, who look for the entire world like little Chinese dolls that I remember from my extreme youth. They seemed happy and contented and oddly naive and unselfconscious. Most of them wore shawls and highly coloured beads and sometimes a version of the Indian sari. Apparently one can wear exactly what one fancies as regards a hat. They were delightfully varied and cosmopolitan throughout.

It was cold enough when we actually arrived and, after rickshawing it up and down and uphill again to the Windermere and not being sure of accommodation, we transferred ourselves to Mount Everest, where we were sure of a roof over our heads. We had rooms overlooking the 'snows' – at least the hotel authorities said so – mine did certainly, but Bob's, with the exception of about two inches in one corner, overlooked the well next door. Anyway, we were extremely lucky throughout and even the weather, although not always clear, didn't deter us from enjoying ourselves. We had fires in our rooms day and night and how we needed them. It was so lovely to come in after the cinema at night, cold and breathless after the last climb up the drive, to turn the key in the lock and to see the fire burning brightly in the grate and feel the warmth leaping out to greet us.

We usually spent the mornings walking aimlessly and doing odd bits of shopping and got back in time for lunch. After tiffin we would draw up the sofa in front of the fire and have a sleep until teatime. At first we started to make toast at the fire and started seriously to collect butter for it, keeping what was left from breakfast and so on, but then we discovered delicious sausage rolls in the village and from then on we heated them up daily, in readiness for 4pm, when the bearer would enter with the tea tray. He always tiptoed in but immediately proceeded to knock things over as soon as he arrived. He had attached himself to Bob at the station and proved reliable and very helpful. After tea we sallied forth to the cinema – every night except Sunday, when we went to church! Usually the show was quite good and the place was always full of Tommies who saw all the jokes. Then the long climb home again in the cold night air and uphill all the way. Bob had found the elevation trying for the first week but I didn't notice it. Unfortunately, I was unable to get any films at all, so couldn't take any snaps with my camera – and just when I most wanted them. But we were able to buy very good photos of Darjeeling and the mountains, but then they have nothing personal about them. I was disappointed.

Kanchenjunga was a grand sight on days when it was clear – usually early in the morning while we were having breakfast. I shall never forget the first morning when I went across to the window – there it was looming so closely I felt I could lean out of the window and touch it. The eternal snows – how they must have intrigued and exasperated travellers and explorers and painters and poets of all ages. Always there, if not always to be seen. Sometimes the green valley below was full of woolly clouds like a great sea with the peaks standing crystal clear and sunlit above them; sometimes they would vanish completely as though they had been some product of the imagination. Always it seemed like some far fair promised land, ever beckoning, tantalizing and luring one on to find it. How I would have loved to follow on 'beyond that last great mountain capped with snow' away into Tibet, far from wars and the army. Then, the last evening, as we stood at the window and watched the sunset – the valley clouded and most of the mountains obscured – the very tips of the furthest peaks were clearer, standing out and glowing in the setting sun. It was a lovely last glimpse of those great mountains that maybe neither of us shall see again. We had had a fortnight there – completely removed from the maddening crowd – and returned to Calcutta early on Wednesday morning. I stayed in town that night as I wasn't due back on duty until the Friday.

I saw Bob off on the train on Thursday evening bound for Bombay and Basrah. That's a week ago now and it seems like a dream already that he has been and gone his way again. Now everything seems flat and uninspiring and I have a definite feeling that something is missing. I went to D1 for the first few days but appear to have come to roost for the moment in E2, with Watson. It's pleasant there – quiet and tucked away and no one bothers us.

I have discovered a Welshman – a minister's son – from Pembrokeshire in H Ward (TB) and he has a friend, Davies, from Portmadog who is a patient in one of the other wards. They are an interesting pair. Davies is mixed up with the Welsh National Theatre and knows many people that I knew once upon a time. Like a breath of fresh air from the Caernarvonshire hills, it is, to talk about the old spots again. But it fills me with 'hiraeth'[67] all over again and I am not sure it is good for me.

There have been letters from Gwen, Mali and Ruthin cousins this week and one from Mother. It seems that sister Mona has been appointed leading lady in *Night Must Fall*.[68] They must be busy, wherever they are doing their war service; at all events she must have some more energy than I have. I'm in the throes of a wretched cold, which is rather shocking just on top of a month's leave. The weather is still very lovely, warm in the sun and the nights are cool, not cold.

The war news remains good: Kursk re-taken by the Russians and the Solomons evacuated by the Japanese. Oh, if only it would all finish soon!

June 19th 1943

What a shocking lapse and so much, so very much has happened in the interim that I just can't think where to begin. To begin with for instance, I am married. Even as I write it, I rather wonder if it is true – but I have my marriage certificate so I suppose I haven't dreamed it. Also I distinctly remember saying, 'I do' rather remotely and nervously and hearing David say the same, even more so as he stood beside me. That was on May 20th, a little over a month ago, and David is long ago back among the flying things and I am endeavouring to run the staff, nurse the patients and control the equipment on my large and difficult ward, Surgery A – BMH. I left Loreto to do night duty about three months ago and I have remained here since, living in my more sane moments in No. 5 Minto Park.

Mona, very nobly, came all the way from Dehra Dun to lend me moral support on my wedding day. David had come down the previous Sunday. What a week that was in Calcutta: a taxi strike and a water strike. We had to gharry or rickshaw everywhere. And whereas at one stage in my life, I might have considered it highly diverting and delightful to be conveyed thus to my destination, the idea of arriving thus at the church door on my wedding day definitely had no appeal. Geoffrey Holland arrived that day with no less than two beautiful gharries complete with the usual weary and disillusioned-looking horses, having captured them triumphantly at Enbally and brought them all the way for the purpose. However at the very last moment David had managed to enlist the sympathy of an RAF padre who conveyed each of us in turn safely and comfortably to the appointed place in his camouflaged car. I have never appreciated the ordinary motor car as a means of transport until this occasion. The water problem, which was desperate indeed – I loathed washing piecemeal any time and go breakfast-less daily in order to have my morning bath – was solved at the eleventh hour, when the taps decided to run. So I was saved the indignity of having to proceed to my wedding unwashed!

Those present included Mona, Geoffrey (who gave me away), and Edward Selwyn who supported David and duly handed over the wedding ring at the right moment, and Vera

Fairweather and the RAF padre: a small but select party. It was a simple service – short and rather beautiful and I think even Dafydd,[69] who doesn't altogether love churches, was also moved. We went on to the Great Eastern Hotel and had drinks and then lunch. There were one or two little speeches, which I'd like to have remembered, but have not. Then we went our several ways, David and I taking up our abode in the Victoria Hotel for the remainder of my leave, which was altogether one week. It was pleasant there and comparatively cool and airy.

Edward came to lunch and to dine with us a few times and Geoffrey came – very preoccupied with prickly heat – to tea on the last afternoon. Dafydd and I distinguished ourselves by 'allowing' a light to shine forth from the bathroom window on the last night. There was a pane of glass missing – it had been so for nine months or so it seems – and it was spotted by the police at last. The management seemed upset but I didn't give it another thought as I considered it entirely their affair, but a day or so ago a detective walked in and opened up the subject again. It was rather amazing as they suspected a first-rate mystery and had had five men on the job for more than three weeks. I have to go and see the Commissioner of Securities and tell him my story. I didn't tell him, as I should like to have done, that the manager of the Victoria Hotel had followed the detective that afternoon and had asked me to back up his miserable story that we had 'removed the shade from the light'. He nearly wept, saying that he would lose his job and so on, but I told him that he should have thought of that before. He agreed. Furthermore, unfortunately, David had signed D.H. Davies in the civilian register, although that was their fault, of course, as they knew perfectly well that he was in the RAF. I've heard nothing more so I presume that the matter has been settled 'out of court'.

There were one or two incidents – amusing now – one at the close of the following Sunday morning service and resulting in a waste paper basket full of torn up manuscripts: such a waste of paper and time. Poor David!

And now we are both back at our jobs again and the monsoons are breaking – half-heartedly as yet – and the heat is still around and about us and altogether life isn't *comme il faut*. However, there are compensations – letters arrive fairly well and the frangipani still blooms and the poinsettias have been a perfect glory – like a hundred burning bushes on Chowringhee and in the garden of Minto Park. Convoys come in – and go out, almost as quickly: hospital ships, troopships and ambulance trains bringing boys down from Burma, where something still goes on – presumably.

The Middle East of course is finished[70] and everyone waits breathlessly for news of a 'second front'. Clwyd has actually been home for a month's leave and sister Mona was able to join him, from the second AGH in the tablelands of Queensland. Clwyd is now an S/Sgt, Glyn a bombardier and stationed somewhere near Sydney. Mali and Gwen write regularly and I write not so regularly to them and occasionally to others. I drift on in a state of semi-coma from day to day and what I do with my alternate half-days, I couldn't rightly say. Waste them – it is to be presumed.

I am writing this on a 10–1 shift, and a moment ago my bearer came up and said that a 'soldier sahib' wanted to see me. It was a sergeant with a Welsh accent whom I didn't know. He told me that he was Miss Timothy's nephew (shades of Llanerch Road) and that a S/Sgt Lewis, whose wife knew me once upon a time, wanted to call and see me, but 'didn't like to' for some reason. I can't think who she used to be but I told the boy to tell him to call just the same.

And now its 12 midday and I must change my uniform and proceed to lunch.

June 27th 1943

A half-day and as is becoming usual these days, I got down on my bed until 4pm and then went downstairs for tea. Since then I have been writing to David. Edward called for a moment, and we made arrangements to meet for lunch – all three of us at Christies, on the 14th.

How tired I am these days. It amazes me when I consider myself three years ago and the energy I then possessed and how little I can muster now. It irritates me too; in three years I haven't become appreciably older and I should still be capable of a good day's work. Now, with a half-day off on alternate days, I feel mentally and physically worn out. This monsoon weather is rather depressing, we all feel that, but it is really the war that gets on top of me. I won't talk about it here; I have it around and about me all day and that is more than enough. I long for a quiet hill station; nothing spectacular at all, removed from all excitement and glamour. It would revive me, I know. The Eastern Army did a round at 10.30 today – Sunday – notwithstanding the usual nonsense and all patients wearing red ties and at their beds, looking sheepish and silly. I had to take the senior man around and tell him what was what, while the CO and Matron and numerous lesser lights such as brigadier generals and full colonels and all their satellites, not to mention our own MOs, trailed languidly behind. Such a waste of time although, I admit, it is why on these occasions, one can get anything done on a ward.

July 1st 1943

July – I can't believe it. How the months slip by; the second half of the year now – and yesterday it seems I was writing 1942.

I had a remarkable letter from David yesterday, regarding an American function I had promised to attend, as one of ten from the BGH. Some time back I had been told of a Welsh concert at the YWCA and had at once decided to attend that instead (ah me, 'what mighty contents arise from trivial things?'). But tonight – tonight is golden – the palms stand straight and tall and unstirring against the setting sun. Here at least, there is nothing to jar, to irritate or to disillusion the unquiet spirit. I have just finished reading and enjoyed Osbert Sitwell's *Open The Door*. The radio is pouring out some unknown symphony and through my still open shutters I can see the crows flying home to rest in the mango trees on the lawns below.

July 3rd 1943

Just another half-day and *c'est tout*!

July 18th 1943

David has been and gone his ways again. He had 48 hours travelling time in order to see his play produced and broadcast on the radio. I went to Sealdah station to meet him and arrived at 8.30, the supposed time of arrival. The train – labelled simply 'Burarah' – ambled into the dark station about 9.25pm with no murmur or apology for my long wait. These Indian stations always seem to be crowded with sleeping half-naked bodies day and night, it's just the same. I believe I was the only European there among them. I sat in the shadows on a seat alongside an Indian gentleman – caste unknown – with a large black monsoon umbrella. I wondered what was passing through his mind as he sat there immovable, inscrutable, amid all these heaps of rags in diverse postures covering, or making some pretence of covering, some miserable forms of humanity. Although one is used to it long since and often does not even notice such a scene at all, or think it unusual, there are still occasions when it strikes the eye and an impression is left indelibly upon the mind. Then at such times, I long to be able to paint it all – I feel that there are no words for it. There is a mix of glamour and pathos about the East – the colour, the sounds, even the evil smells: all life is there.

Then the great searchlight on the front of the train appeared around the bend and at once the whole station was alive again. The forms that looked like bundles of filthy rags, sprang up and ran – ran anywhere – up and down the platform, screaming and pushing, arguing and gesticulating. I wondered idly if most of their lives were spent like this, day after day, night after night. And while I pitied them, I half envied them – untroubled as they are with possessions, ambitions or hopes. They have nothing and I do not doubt that they hope for nothing. With a shrug of the shoulders they go on existing from day to day and on the last day of their lives they go to join the sea that 'gathers all things unto itself'.

I saw David from far off, tall and lean in a large Mackintosh cape and topee: a curious combination in anyone else but Dafydd. Although I had sent two wires to say I would meet him, he hadn't received either and must have wondered as to whether I would be there. We got a taxi then to Fairlawns and then went out to a nearby Chinese restaurant and had some dinner. It was a small pokey room at the hotel into which, it seemed, they had pushed at the last moment, a second bed; still it was a room and it served. Someone with a curiously diverse taste in music played Grieg and the latest jazz alternately so after being transported into a rarefied state during *Peer Gynt*, we were driven to despair by the latest hit song. We continued to eat dinner there twice and the service was so superb that we romped through about six courses in about as many minutes. Ray Conaughton and his delightful Indian girl Oomah ate with us one night – the night of the play. We collected some of the cast for BESA[71] still dressed as they appeared in the show and proceeded to the radio centre where Edward was already. I sat in a room apart and listened and David joined me as soon as he had said his lines. Edward and Mary were really splendid but Annie was a sad disappointment. She romped through her lines and her voice was too shrill and unsympathetic. All the while, however, I believe David was well satisfied with it. He's had so little time with them, less than an hour altogether, so that it was amazingly good really. David gets 25 chips – all of it – for this effort and that goes to start a sinking fund – for holidays and such – or so we fondly hope.

I had to get up early next morning, before six, and get myself back to the mess in a rickshaw, there being no taxis about, and in the pouring rain. It was my half-day (I stole the previous one and got away with it for once) and returned to Fairlawns soon after 2pm. David was OUT, had slept until 12.30 and then proceeded to take himself into Park Street to have his photograph taken. He returned later with a cake and a copy of Byron, which it transpired was for me and for which I was ungracious enough to say it did not particularly interest me. He changed it later for a complete W.H. Davies which pleased me much. We spent the evening indoors and returned at midnight, the rain still streaming down, in a rickshaw bound for Minto Park. The poor willing rickshaw driver panted and strained in the rain and all his and David's frantic cry for a taxi proved pointless. The rain seeped down through the hood and trickled down our legs and we were cramped and damp and chastened in spirit. David got a lift back by taxi fortunately and I do hope he managed to get another as he was to leave about 3am, an ungodly hour to embark on that dreary journey. I was as sorry about it as I know very well how he hates Chittagong and everyone in it or near it in his present state of mind. It is too bad that he cannot be posted elsewhere, if not Calcutta, and given some work to do of real interest to him. However, we'll see.

And now the second offensive has begun. The Allies are installed in Sicily and gaining a grip daily, or so we are assured. One presumes that something will start on this front after the rains are over. David thinks his crowd will end up in China. Odd that we can say it and write it and accept it as though one were to say, 'I may be going to the races next week.' Will there be anything left to fill us with wonder and surprise, when all this is over? I doubt it. Well if it is China, it is a dreary prospect: irregular mail, so little hope of an odd meeting, so many months of wondering and worrying. I try to live beyond all this, to get beyond the unsatisfactory present, to be patient, to accept it all with some semblance of reason and grace. Sometimes I can, but most often, I can't.

The ward still worries me although not as much as it did. But last night I had one of my bad dreams again. I was distinctly awake. I could see the palms outside my window and the light shone across the floor from the next door room and then I felt it approach – this unseen, formless, dreadful 'something' that literally drags me in two, leaving my physical conscious body where it is, speechless and powerless to move, whilst sometimes I am propelled through space as though expelled by some unseen evil power. I hear voices, many voices, excited and jabbering incoherently – which always occurs – and last night I thought someone came and knocked at my door and wanted to give me a message. I watched the door frantically, hoping they would come in, but although I tried to call out that I was there, I had no power to speak at all.

Later Vera came in wearing evening dress as she had gone out some hours before and I tried, I thought, to speak to her.

I hoped that she would see that my eyes were open and that she would speak to me; she said something and that broke that awful spell. I made myself speak to her and she put the light on and gave me a cigarette and I had a drink and told her about it and how thankful I was that she had come in. At such times I feel I shall never be able to drag myself to acute consciousness again. I seem to be possessed, body and mind, by this awful power. What I am afraid of is that I shall dread going to sleep at all, in case it appears again. I had some aspirin and vegamins and eventually slept quite well, except for the usual dreaming which I always do. I felt quite tattered and worn out this morning, but I am better again now.

Sometimes I think that I will ask to be posted elsewhere – it would take my mind off many things. A change of environment would give a fresh interest and heart. But then I feel, while David is at least comparatively near Calcutta, it would be a pity for me to be moved somewhere inaccessible, particularly as he may move beyond all hope of meeting, as time goes on.

It is 7.30pm, the hour when my bearer brings me my coffee as I never go to supper. Night is falling fast as it does in the east and soon I shall close the shutters and employ myself somehow until it is time to fall into my little camp bed. I was talking to Golightly today (who was with us at 92 Cromwell Road) and she told me that of the five girls who went forth from Millbank to Singapore, she is the only one who escaped. Two definitely were killed by direct hits on the hospital and the other two are prisoners, if indeed they are still alive. I often think what a strange and tragic tale it would be, if one could know the details of all the lives that went out from the club in those far off days in August 1940. How little any of us suspected what lay before us in those days of boredom and waiting. And now …

August 3rd 1943

Three years ago on this very day we slipped out of the Mersey, under cover of night; destroyers and cruisers to guard us with the rest of that large convoy. So much has happened since then – so much.

I am so tired again; any hour is just at a standstill but relief is on its way. I feel like a prisoner who has been told his reprieve is at hand. I think I have had in the last four months the worst collection of orderlies in the whole British Army. With a very few exceptions I must regretfully put it on record that the RAMC (orderlies) is not worth its salt in this war. For lack of intelligence, interest, co-operation it would be difficult to find its equal. I think it must indeed be true that those who are totally unfit for any other kind of war service are pushed into its ranks.

August 9th 1943

Just as I was writing the above complaint, Alsander came in and begged me to join a party at the Club. I said, 'No, definitely no' and meant it; but she seemed desperate as she had promised to rope in someone else, and in the end I got myself drawn in and went. I was glad in the end because it took me out of myself and life is dull enough at present. It's all a matter of filling in time and I suppose one must just make the best of it. There was a regular army captain among the crowd and, as his views on India and imperialism weren't exactly mine, we had plenty of scope for a discussion. I got some support for once too – and from a Scot. The poor man must have felt rather bewildered at the attack; for I am sure he has never been crossed before, on this question, which most people accept as 'divine right'. There was a very right-thinking American civilian amongst them (we went to his flat first) whose wife is interned in one of the Japanese occupied islands. It is rare to meet a Calcutta civilian who isn't thoroughly biased about the Indians.

I've handed over A to Standing now. I had a 'barrack equipment' check one afternoon and the very next morning had to trot everything out again, much to my displeasure. On the whole I didn't do so badly, for in four months I lost only:

Pails, slop 1 (one)
Ewers, enamel 1 (one)
Syringe, Higginson 1 (one)
Probe 1 (one)
Counter scissors 1 (one)
Sheets 30 (thirty).

It doesn't look so good in the 'handing-over book' in Matron's office but so relieved and exultant was I that I had got rid of it all, I shouldn't have cared if the list were ten times as long.

I shall be leaving the army soon so have agreed to work on ambulance trains in the meantime. But the floods have held things up and few trains are running anywhere so it may be weeks yet. Meanwhile I remain on A Ward as a mere subsidiary, where for so long, I held complete control. I don't like it very much, but it is better than having the worry of it all.

I've had a chit from the Chartered Bank to the effect that someone owes me £5, which translated means around 60 chips. It comes through the Commonwealth Bank of Australia, Sydney. It's from someone in the family – perhaps – nice of whomsoever it was anyway. I'm poor this month as it happens, the field cashier having cheerfully taken 600 chips from me for July, leaving me without an anna. I wish they wouldn't be so ruthless in their deductions. If 'they' take 200 a month I might get out of debt to them one day. As it is, I visit the fort every month and draw another 200 to keep the wolf from the door. Taxis have increased their flag fares to one rupee instead of eight annas: 1/6 for a few yards seems a bit too much. One could so easily walk, but it is either too hot to drag oneself around or it rains so heavily, as it is doing today and did yesterday, that a taxi seems the only means of rescue from death by drowning. The roof in 'A' has been leaking badly again and everywhere one walks there is a pool of water or a bucket or basin. Going across on duty yesterday, I completely ruined my comfortable white duty shoes, wading through a rushing torrent past my ankles. There was no path to be seen anywhere and I had to go on duty, of course. It's a dreary afternoon – my half-day – and I sit in this untidy room trying to while away the hours until I get up tomorrow morning. It's the waste of time that I so deplore – I just can't settle to anything worthwhile.

August 26th 1943

Ambulance Train BN Line

I should have written this before, of course, for this is my second and last trip and we are now on the run home – somewhere between Midnapur and Howrah. The first time we were away eight days, disgorging patients en route at Ranchi, Lucknow, Biralli and finally Dehra Dun. At first I hated it – the dust and train grime, the eternal chug chugging of the wheels, the constant rocking motion of the carriages, the confined space, worse than the ship, but gradually I became used to it and, surprisingly enough, have ended up liking it. Not, I know, that I should like it for long – but it was a relief to be away from the wards, the maddening routine of doing dressings and giving out medicine and writing reports. A relief, too, to be out of the mess, the idle gossip, the talk of the shop, the irritating remarks at the table, the neverending enveloping atmosphere of a hospital. True, this was uninteresting as regards work, but the scene was fresh and the paddy fields green, and there were occasional brightly coloured birds, and the long-legged elegant cranes stalking through the flood waters, and there was an amusing colony of monkeys, which as one man came alongside the train when it stopped, begged for food – imitating no doubt the eternal railway station beggar who, in India, is legion. I read with interest and without interruption and I played my records over and over again.

I couldn't contact Mona in Dehra Dun as there was no time but it looked a delightful place and I envied her green and delightful surroundings. The days in Lucknow on the return run resulted in an almost empty purse, for things were attractive and different and cheaper than in Calcutta. And so by easy stages, very easy, we ambled back into Howrah. I had a young Anglo-Indian girl with me, very attractive and a good companion. She amused and annoyed me by her attitude towards all Indians; she spoke of them always with complete and utter disgust. She was as Oriental as any Yasmin; her mother was Canadian and her father an Anglo-Indian 'but', she went on, 'only because he had always lived here'. Evidently, she's been told and believes that she has no Indian blood at all, but her looks belie her. She was more attractive for her Indian blood if she only knew it, poor child, than she would have been if she'd been pure European: little and graceful as a kitten. I loved to sit back and watch her move and talk, however stupidly.

I reported back at the mess next day, telling them that I might go again at any time. I lay very low in case Matron decided to put me on duty, and I got away with it. I had three days there but I doubt if she realised it. I came back to the train again yesterday, only to hear we were doing a very short trip this time into Midnapur only ten miles distance and that we would be returning next day. I was sorry, as I still thought I might contact Mona this time with better luck. But there it is and now we are slowly on our way home again, and I shall have to return to the mess tonight.

In the last bundle of letters from home came the news of sister Mona's engagement. I wasn't so surprised but these things always come as a shock, when they are announced and one has been far away for a long time. So both of us leave the parental roof, officially, in one year. I am awfully pleased for her as she will make an excellent wife (in the way that I shall not) and it all sounds very delightful and interesting. How very differently our paths will lie, hers and mine, I well know. We used to say, she and I, that one day we'd buy an old cottage in Surrey and have a garden; we were influenced in our choice of a county by some books we were then reading. Well, a lot of water has flowed under the bridge since then but now I expect she will live in Melbourne, while I, having at times considered living in various spots on earth, will have returned to my native hills. *Ainsi soit-il!*

But for now it is still India and just at the moment rather pleasant countryside – scattered native villages, thatched roofs, mud huts, clumps of palms, long water lily-covered lagoons, or whatever they are called here, brown bodies bathing among the reeds, cows and goats grazing quietly in the fields. It looks quiet and peaceful and far removed from all the complexity and worries of the sophisticated city.

Sometimes I envy these simple people for their detachment, their aimlessness and their lack of responsibility. The fact that we consider that they are missing so much that we consider essential, what of it? Perhaps they would not understand it anyway and they would be more than fools if they desired it:

Let not ambition mock their useful toil
Their homely joys and destiny obscure.[72]

September 29th 1943

This is becoming a monthly affair of late and scarcely a record of activities, if such a word is applicable in these monotonous days. I got back from the train in time for Vera's wedding to Patrick. She looked very sweet in a blue suit and Blandie wore navy blue. St Paul's was nicely decorated and the whole unit turned out in strength and the CO gave her away. The reception was held in the mess and it was quite a large affair and all were very happy and jolly. We went to see them off on the Darjeeling mail in the evening; the carriage was duly decorated and petals were carefully sprinkled over everything, for atmosphere. Then we went on to spend the rest of the evening at the Nan King and ate curries, delicious Chinese dishes and the MOs did tricks with their glasses, all very undignified, but there was a lot of cheer and good humour.

I was at Davidian Schools then for a week or so until I went 'on nights' in Officers Surgical. That was pleasant and I was enjoying it when, much to my disgust, I had to go off sick with dengue again. I was warded this time in Sick Sisters for a week and then I had four days off in Minto Park. When I returned on duty it was to C Ward until I was due to return for the rest of my night duty, this time to B, where I write this. Anything that has legs or wings or any life at all in the insect world is on my table tonight – the most curious looking creatures. The lizards on the wall are having a royal feast. One has just attacked successfully a great strapping grasshopper, head on, and proceeded to swallow it in six gulps. I watched it, intrigued, and after about thirty seconds, it had a series of abdominal convulsions and the whole thing came back up again – intact – but the lizard, evidently a lizard of some determination, started swallowing it all over again and, it appears, this time it remained where it was first meant to go. It is quiet here at present, no one is very ill (about

100 patients) and the only hectic period is between 5 and 8am, for we have to make the most of the beds. Anyway, the days are passing and I come off on the 8th October.

That, on the surface, is the sum of my activities over the last month. But alas, I've had more on my mind than just these routine things. For David has sprue and is in hospital in Dacca.[73] He was in Chittagong first, being treated for amoebic dysentery – but later diagnosed as sprue and evacuated to Dacca. Poor David, he had been so unbearably depressed and miserable for so long, it must have been almost a relief for him to be put in hospital at last. But sprue … I can remember every morning when I wakened up, SPRUE seemed to be written across my brain. I could visualize the long months of hospital – perhaps one after another, a mere patient, scarcely an individual at all, and I was fearful for the awful depression and weariness that comes with a long illness, on his mind. One can so easily let go on these occasions and I felt that it might be too much for him. But I feel better about it now, now that I know he is getting good treatment and that someone is interested in him. I wrote to Dorrington and she assured me that the medical specialists there say his cure will be final and that there will be no after-effects.

David himself seems (or seemed), so much more cheerful, so glad to get away from his environment, that the old urge to read and write had returned and an entirely new vista opened up, so that we felt, perhaps this is a good thing after all, here is a way, perhaps the only way, to get him away from all those things he so hated. But the last two letters show a marked decline in spirit again, due perhaps to his injections (liver) and other treatment. He has developed a phobia towards needles which is getting him down. He is beginning to realise now, just how weak he is, that the convalescence will be long and dreary and he just doesn't know what he wants. I can go up to Dacca for my nights off – it will mean only a few hours there, but I must see him for myself and feel it will cheer him up a little. Also, I want to take the gramophone as he needs it more than I do.

It's a bad start off but I am determined not to harp on about it too much. These are trying days and letters are such poor things after all, moody as each one of us is, the smallest situation is bound to be over-emphasised and it takes weeks to disentangle a loosely written phrase. Once we can begin our lives in a normal place together, I shall have no fears at all, but sadly enough I see no prospect of this for many a long day. However, one lives from week to week, undisturbed on the surface, and hoping fervently for the best in one's mind. One day I hope I shall read this and smile to think that I was so foolish to worry myself for nothing.

There's to be a mock air raid in a few minutes – to try out the city's services, I suppose. One has almost forgotten what a siren sounds like; it is so long since its blood-curdling wail was heard hereabouts last Christmas!

Letters from home drift in occasionally – one from Mother about two weeks ago but then there are large gaps and some, even many I am bound to think, do not arrive. Mali and Gwen write faithfully, and the *JOLs* and *Horizons* and *World Reviews* arrive from time to time, delighting me first and then David. *The Captain's Wife*, which Mali sent me, was like a cool breeze after a hot airless day – lovely, lovely, lovely.

There is a pure white moth propelling itself around my books as I write this, about a third of an inch long, with one tiny black eye and long feelers. It gleams like silver and is too pretty a thing to dispatch in the usual way. So because it is beautiful I shall allow it to live its allotted span. If it were ugly, and it displeased me, I suppose I should kill it without a moment's thought. An uncomfortable thought indeed and so true of life!

November 17th 1943

Harrington Street B Floor

Night duty when I last wrote herein and much has happened since. I have seen David – but not in Dacca – that was cancelled at the last minute as he wired to say he was being evacuated, to Dehra Dun. After a fortnight of wondering what was happening, hearing that he had started off in a river steamer and then spent some days in transit, at Seraj Sange, I had a wire to say he had reached Dehra Dun. I was delighted to know he had gone there rather than Biralli or Lucknow, but sad that I had missed him passing through, and that he had not come here to La Martiniere. About three days later, quite late in the evening, I had another wire saying: 'Have been recommended invaliding home. Imperative I see you before Board takes place. Can you come to Dehra Dun immediately?' So I went – starting off at 7.40 for Howrah on a Friday and reaching there about 4pm on a Sunday afternoon. I took a tonga out to the hospital and just as I was nearing the mess, Mona hailed me from the gardens, where she and David were having tea under the trees. To my horror he had a stick and was walking lame and then I learned that, owing to a vitamin B deficiency, he had wasting of the exterior muscle of one leg, a dropped foot and loss of sensation. I saw Colonel Thuraton next morning and he assured me that everything would become normal once he got home and that there was no need to worry. Poor darling, he looked so thin but swore he was much better, although it was very obvious he was still far from well.

I had a room next to Mona and it was delightful there in the sunny compound. The quietness and the complete absence of planes and taxis and cars were as balm to my soul. The gardens were a delight and the lovely hills which surround that place made me long to be home again. I had four full days there and we had tea in the gardens daily on the grass or under the trees. The gramophone came too and it was good to see David come to life again during the *Unfinished Symphony*. I think he realised then that the illness was a superimposed thing after all and that when it passed, everything was intact underneath, and it was a great relief to him and to me.

I left on Thursday evening and arrived at Howrah on Saturday about 8pm. We crossed the flooded areas where 20,000 people had lost their lives and the lines were still down after three months. An incredible sight. A monkey came abroad and stole my complete bunch of bananas when I was out of the train having lunch at one station. I had pleasant companions all the way but the second night was very interrupted with Indians who came and went all through the night. We had a large breakfast at 9 the next morning and then nothing until about 4pm: that was tea and toast which had to be consumed in about five minutes so we were ready for a meal when we arrived back. I returned to Harrington Street to my cholera patient to find another one as well. Both did very well eventually.

David, all this time, was sceptical about his Board passing him, although the CO seemed in no doubt at all. Anyway, it has gone through and he has now arrived in Bombay and awaits his ship.

It's a queer feeling to think everything has changed so within these last three months. Before – one thought of dragging rather drearily on in India until the end of the war. Now the whole face of things has altered entirely and wonderful and unimagined vistas have opened up instead.

I am afraid that I can't get more leave to go to Bombay to see David before he leaves as we are short-staffed and are busy with an influx of malaria cases again. My application has gone to the Principal Matron and I still await a reply. David has written himself, so perhaps I shall hear something soon. I feel so sorry that I cannot give him any definite assurance before he goes but I am certain that I shall get back within a reasonable time. I am buying linen and such things, difficult to get at home, with a view to future days. I can't think of anything else now but the day I arrive in the UK. It's unbelievable when I have been away so long.

It is perfect weather here now – cold nights and chilly mornings and warm lazy days. The humidity has gone entirely.

Christmas arrangements are in full swing. The mess dance is on December 22nd and our Xmas dinner about 27th, after the patients have had theirs and the MOs are having their dance in the first week of the New Year. It is good fun at Xmas on the wards and decorations have already begun.

There has been very little news from home: Clwyd is still in Melbourne; Mona is still in Queensland and Glyn in New South Wales. Mother had flu when she wrote and seemed rather miserable with it. They didn't know when I last wrote that David was ill; it seems fantastic that the mail takes so long coming and going.

As I write the siren goes – the first time since last December – and the planes are overhead though we can't see them and anti-aircraft fire is making a fearful din in the calm of a Sunday morning. Signs of the times, I expect, with more to follow over Xmas.

1944

Bombay – Calcutta – Wales

January 23rd 1944

And so it has come to this: I sit here not very patiently, I admit, and await the word 'Go'! The Indian phase is nearing its close and although I go with mixed feelings, for there is much here that I love and shall miss, I know with absolute certainty that I am glad to be going and that I would not have it any other way. But to go back six weeks – I went to Bombay to see David off in the end. He rang me up one day when I was on duty in Harrington Street, ostensibly to say goodbye. I knew then that I must make a desperate effort to see him before he left and so I went to Matron – knowing that we were less busy and better staffed just then – and she said I could go. I think I was very near to getting a seat on an RAF plane but the registrar spoiled all that and I had the usual long and boring train journey after all plus the expense which, as usual, I could ill afford. And as usual, of course, no one knew the time of the arrival of the train within about four hours but fortunately David was there and all was well. He looked fairly well but tired very easily with walking as I quickly realised. I stayed with Mona's friends the De Muires, where David had already established himself and they had been extraordinarily kind to him. It was a large and pleasant house above Malabar Hill and it was grand to become civilians again and out of the services for a few short days. We came and went as we pleased and, in spite of Mona's added presence, we did manage to have a few hours to ourselves. I was so glad I was able to have those few days and we both felt so much happier about everything in the light of perhaps – we didn't know – a long separation.

I got back to C floor on the 20th to find B floor in Harrington Street in isolation for smallpox. We had 33 patients for those weeks, all fed on the ward, and, as none of them was ill and quite 25 of them could have been discharged, there was little to do except feed them. It was grand fun on Xmas day, in spite of the fact that three of our orderlies had drunk so well and so unwisely, that they were totally useless by midday. The patients came into the kitchen and served their own supper and everything went with a grand spirit. Sally and I were presented with a handbag each and a box of chocolates and flowers and altogether it was quite a family party. I didn't go out on Xmas eve, preferring to stay on until about 1am for the night sister. The unit dance was a great success at Loreto on the 23rd and on New Year's Eve there was the usual Braces club party at the Chinese restaurant, followed by an hour at the pantomime ending up in a frantic rush to get to Jimmy's flat before midnight to see the New Year in. We didn't make it actually, in spite of considerable abuse, in our best Hindustani, to the taxi driver. But we turned all the clocks in the flat back, and started all over again. The CO's dance started with dinner in the Great Eastern, given by Mac, of all people. It was very hilarious – the champagne probably – and Mac was persuaded to ascend the platform and sing *Danny Boy*, his theme song, and for the rest of the time the orchestra played Irish airs, believing us to be an Irish party, I presume.

I was fairly drunk before I had drunk anything at all, because I had had the news that day that I was to be transferred to Colaba to wait a duty passage home. I didn't, I regret to say, remember much about the rest of the night except that it was an occasion for much good will and toasts on my behalf and everybody telling me how glad they were. We got to Loreto somehow in Jimmy's car and we were told that the dance that had been fairly dull up to that point had brightened up after our arrival. I shouldn't wonder.

A few nights after that the Brace's club farewelled me again, first at Jimmy's flat *avec* the Matron and Colonel Jones and later at the Chinese restaurant. Vera had by this time just discovered that she could be repatriated and Patrick had decided that it would be better for her to go. I am sorry I can't remember the speeches, especially Johnnie's delivered in best Churchillian-cum-Roosevelt manner: they were gems. The prawns, as usual, were excellent and I regret to say that I ate far too many at the instigation of Johnnie who kept telling me that that every prawn might be my last for years. I thought that that would be my last – positively my last appearance at those happy but mad dinners – but Johnnie Hall was expecting to be posted to Japan the next week and, of course, that was an excuse for another one. This one ended rather abruptly with Jimmy being driven home in his own car by Willie Thompson who was distinctly more sober. We went down next day to see Johnnie off and, although I very definitely meant to go back to my packing immediately after, somehow or other we ended up for lunch at the Stafi and they all came to the Minto Park afterwards and insisted on staying for tea. In the hour they had to spare they climbed up poles and palm trees and jumped the dahlia beds and altogether behaved like naughty boys.

I've forgotten to mention that Mona bussed up with her unit about a week before I left and she kept appearing at some time every day. We had dinner with Padre Thompson one night and I took her with me to say goodbye to Ray and Oomah.

I was off the two days previous to my departure and although I'd been packing for days – it still haunts me – much of it couldn't be done until the last day. My warrant and orders were handed to me duly and I was to leave by the Bombay Mail on the Monday evening. Well – I didn't. I was so certain that I knew the time of the departure of the Bombay Mail that I merely glanced at my orders, without reading them properly. Mona, Vera and Patrick came down in the ambulance with me and Tommy and Mac followed in T's car. I had given myself a full hour to deal with my luggage – but – I discovered to my horror and chagrin on arrival that the Bombay Mail was just steaming slowly but definitely out of the platform. It was a good thing I suppose that I wasn't alone for I certainly would have wanted to sit down and howl – but they were all so good and so helpful and I shall always remember the crowd of us threading our way in and out of the bodies on Howrah station, with Tommy and Mac roaring out, 'A troopship was leaving Bombay,' trying to cheer me up. We installed the luggage in 'the left luggage room' and went off in Jimmy's little car – the men all roaring lustily – to Firpo's.

There in Firpo's we dined and danced for the last time in Calcutta; it was January 1944. After that we went onto the Palo Rica for a while before going home. We delivered Mona safely and I crawled into Minto Park and into Vera's bed for positively the last time. Mona came early next morning and we did some shopping prior to a last lunch with T and M at the Great

Eastern. They had to get back to their work and Mona came down to Howrah with me and saw me safely installed with all my belongings – bound for Bombay – and Blighty.

And so ends my Calcutta interlude. In many ways I felt sad at leaving for I had so many real friends there and I was always happy in the unit. But this, of course, is merely incidental to my life and, in leaving it, I close the door – only too readily – on so many things that are extraneous and quite outside my life and the life I want. So *Vale* Calcutta – Chowringhee, Firpo's, the Great Eastern, Christies, the Nan King, the Slap and all the other haunts – and those names that will become mere memories, I suppose: Vera and Audrey and Margaret and Peggy and Mac and Watson and McNamara and Blondie and Babs and Sally – Patrick and Tommy and Mac and Johnny and Willie and Gay – and Wender and Paddy and Arthur – and as Johnny would say, Uncle John Cobbly and all. They were as grand a collection of friends as anyone could have wished and I am grateful to them all.

But now I am in Bombay – in Colaba – and as restless as a leaf in the wind. I don't, I am afraid, like the matron, who made it definitely clear to me – without any need of words – AC1 was a rank she had never heard of, when I was giving her David's particulars. It enraged me so much that his number went completely out of my head and it wasn't until I had cooled down and I had got back almost to my mess that it came back to me. When I first arrived the girls were having only two and a half days a week, which rather horrified me as I felt I had so much yet to do. Today a notice has gone up saying that we may take every other half-day until further orders. Another thing which has made me cross is that messing here is 100 chips a month. We were on rations of course and paid no more than Rs46. This, in my present financial state, is more than a blow, especially as I never appear for breakfast or dinner. The food is very good, I admit, but it seems entirely unnecessary somehow. The mess itself is quite charming with everything nicely done. I am not in Alexandra House but in a long two-storied bungalow across the road. It has wide verandahed balconies on all sides and is most comfortable. Another girl shares the room with me: it is a large room with real beds and there is a dressing room with three wardrobes and a bathroom off stage. Colaba itself is a huge military compound, covering numerous acres on the sea front, and must 'house' thousands of army and naval personnel of various units. There are churches and cinemas and canteens and halls and barracks and houses (many families of course live within the compound) and altogether it is a complete world in itself.

Much to my surprise in the little time I have had to myself, I have done quite a few of the things that I knew had to be done in case I had to leave quickly. My account has been transferred to Lloyds and I've been to the RAF about my allotment. I quite looked forward to about Rs400, only to find they had already paid Rs315 into Lloyds Calcutta, and as it was exactly the same amount as my December pay, I have naturally concluded that the army had paid me twice over that month. Lloyds mentioned it as 'my salary due for the month of December' and I accepted it gratefully (not too surprised at anything the pay department does, although it is usually the other way round) and felt it was worth having it even if I did have to pay it back later. Well this was rather shattering news and I had to make up my mind that if this was my marriage allotment, then I had had it and spent it – or a good deal of it. They had just sent this month's allowance to Lloyds Chowringhee (Rs64 or thereabouts) and it will be a while before that is transferred to Bombay, I suppose.

I've left my wireless in Calcutta to be disposed of and that should bring Rs500. It probably won't but I'd be mighty glad of this at the moment. There are things I feel I must buy – towels and soap and some warm things for David. I don't mind about things for me, although I do need shoes and other odds and ends. I went out to Mary's flat yesterday afternoon to collect my stuff. Oh, those books: I'll have to get a packing case for them, I'm afraid.

I am so afraid of having to leave in a hurry and without any money. I must keep some for emergencies – taxis and coolies and tips on the ship and such incidentals, and I can't possibly arrive penniless. I wish I didn't worry so much about money. I am not very interested in it as such, but I've learned only too well that we can't be without it. I rather hope, much as I dislike having to settle amongst a new unit, and much as I badly want to get back to David, that I can have a few weeks here and by that time someone may have bought my wireless and that would relieve the situation immensely. I have been on tenterhooks for days, knowing that several ships were going and thinking that I might be pushed on one at the last moment. It's still possible of course but I hope not as I've got some material being made up into grey uniforms and I'd have to leave that behind.

If I have time I must call and see the De Muires with some cheese but apart from that I'm truly thankful that I have no social obligations of any kind in Bombay these days.

February 15th 1944

The time has come – we are about to depart these shores. I have been here almost a month and now it is a matter of days. I had a day off yesterday and spent it laboriously shopping. There are so many things I feel I want to buy, not for myself but for the many others whom I have not seen for so long. I bought some food stuffs but not much as the price was beyond my purse.

The packing has been done for the third time and I am hoping I shall have room for everything. I went to see Mrs De Muires a night or two ago and I must ring Niermol today and tell him that I am about to depart. Mary is coming this evening. And there was a letter from Mali last night in which she sounded so depressed. How wearily the war rages for everyone who is just at home, trying to make things as normal as possible, under trying conditions. We in the services are far better off and, quite unjustifiably, collect the laurels.

And so perhaps in a month's time I shall be at home again. It will be March – wild winds and cold. I shudder to think of it on this bright warm day. Still spring will follow and with it the joy of seeing primroses again and cowslips and daffodils. All this will be at one with yesterday's seven thousand years and just a memory. I wonder where David will be – still in hospital, discharged or at home. I shan't know until I actually arrive back. No cable yet. I should be so depressed if I didn't know that we will be together soon. But it doesn't matter now. This is the last time I shall write herein, overseas: almost four years since I was first posted to the Middle East and a lot of water has flowed under the bridge since then. A rich few years in many ways and I am the wiser for them. Out of all the chaos there are memories of many friendships, precious and dear. And they will outlast the war – I know that. Now I am facing the other way and the beginning of my real life. So many steps, so many curious twists and then one arrives. And now I dare to hope for some permanence at last – a real aim and a steady course – to the end of it all. It may take time but that it will come I do not doubt.

So *Vale* India!

POSTSCRIPT

So what happened after the war?

Joyce and David began their married life in the small village of Llanferres near RAF Sealand before settling in Swansea and then Cardiff from 1955. David became a journalist on South Wales newspapers and continued to pursue his love of theatre by directing plays for Eisteddfodau and amateur theatres before he was appointed as a radio producer (drama) for the BBC in Cardiff. I was the oldest child, born in 1944; Siân was born two years later and our brothers Ifor and Vaughan followed. So by 1950 Joyce, aged 42, was a full-time housewife with four small children and she was 10,500 miles from her family. She never saw her mother, father or sister Mona again and spoke only twice to them on the telephone. Compared to her life in Australia and much of her wartime experience, life after the war was hard: strict rationing, a cold and damp climate, the British diet with the absence of tropical fruit that she loved and the dreariness of the heavily bombed town of Swansea. Despite the post-war deprivations, which were shared by everyone, she was an exceptionally able manager of a large household which often included actors who needed a bed or a meal. And she was an inspiring mother who sought to nurture talents in each of her children: Siân is an illustrator and artist, Ifor a musician and photographer and Vaughan a writer and landscape gardener. She was a much-loved friend to many people and it was she who created the ballast in a rather bohemian household in which well-known actors, writers and painters came and went and where contemporary ideas, books and politics were discussed with great passion. She remained an avid reader and collector of poetry and contemporary fiction, including the emerging Australian writers.

Without our being fully aware at the time, Joyce's war experience was all around us: our playroom had a dark green canvas bed, bucket and washbasin; her double blue tin trunk had the names of every port scrawled or plastered on it and our dressing-up clothes were silk, crêpe de chine or brocade dresses and shoes that she had had made by the dursies on the side of the road in India. And when I found and came to read the journal some sixty years later I found some of the stories that she had told us and the vivid descriptions of places that she had never forgotten.

Despite the interesting and rich family life that she had created, the strains in the marriage and the incompatibility of personalities that were hinted at in the last few months of the journal resulted in divorce after twenty years. Later, Joyce married Dewi-Prys Thomas, Professor of Architecture at Cardiff University and a passionate Welsh Nationalist. They shared a deep love of history, literature and Welsh affairs and travelled together to Greece (which she had never reached in the war), Malta and further afield. She journeyed to Australia in her mid-70s where she was reunited with her brothers, their families and old friends. And in her early 80s, after Dewi's death in 1985, she travelled on her own to Spain, Russia and Samarkand. She lived in the home of Siân and her husband Peter in her last years, from where she took great delight in the interests and successes of her children and her four grandchildren, Catrin, Owain, Lucy and Rhianwen. Joyce died in Birkenhead in 1992 aged 83 and in her last days she was back on the slow train up to Darjeeling, smelling the guavas piled on the stations. Those 'four rich years', as she called her war years, were with her to the end.

Rhiannon Evans
2015

About the Editor

Professor Emeritus Rhiannon Evans was Pro-Vice Chancellor at Edge Hill University until her retirement in 2009. She received an MBE in 2008 for services to higher education, particularly for her national work on widening access. She will finish walking around the 890 miles of the Wales coastal path in 2015 and also hopes to undertake some more of her mother's Indian train journeys. She lives in Birkenhead.

NOTES

1. Antony Beevor, *The Second World War* (Weidenfeld & Nicolson, 2012).
2. The history of the QAIMNS(R) started some twelve years before the outbreak of the First World War during a time of relative peace in the British Empire. The Queen Alexandra's Imperial Military Nursing Service (Reserve), named in honour of Queen Alexandra, replaced the Army Nursing Service and the Indian Nursing Service in 1902 by Royal Warrant. It became known as the QAs.
3. Where she had been in lodgings while nursing in Llandudno.
4. The War Office requested suitably trained nurses to join the QAIMNS(R) in 1938 when war was anticipated. Nurses were interviewed and given sealed packages which bore the words 'Open only in the event of war'.
5. Millbank, next to the Tate Gallery, was the headquarters of the QAIMNS. Now it is the location of Chelsea College of Art and Design.
6. In the margin is written 'Frequent air raid signals in the last week in Le Mans. No one took any notice of them after the first half dozen.'
7. In May the British Expeditionary Force was withdrawn from France, leading up to Dunkirk.
8. Tricolene was a white dress worn by army nurses in the tropics.

9. *The Merchant of Venice*, Act V, Scene 1.
10. Rupert Brooke: 'The Dead'.
11. The beginning of the Blitz and the intense bombing of London and other major cities.
12. Battle of Britain day with the largest attacks on London by 1,500 German aircraft.
13. A guide or interpreter.
14. Saqqara is a vast burial ground serving as the necropolis for the ancient capital of Memphis.
15. Mereruka's tomb is the largest and most elaborate of the non-royal tombs.
16. A fortified place for heavy guns.
17. A felucca is the traditional wooden sailing ship used along the Nile since antiquity. It has two triangular sails and can accommodate up to ten people.
18. It is noted in Tyrer, *Sisters in Arms* (Weidenfeld & Nicolson, 2008) that fraternising between QAs and sergeants was discouraged.
19. A novel by Sir Walter Scott, set in 1187 during the Third Crusade.
20. This refers to November 14th when 400 German bombers attacked the city: 568 people were killed and 100,000 fled the city where 60 per cent of the buildings had been damaged.
21. Used as a cleaning agent.
22. The British begin the Western Desert offensive against the Italians.
23. All sea ports in eastern Libya where the British and Commonwealth forces were in battle with the Italians.
24. A city on the coast of Eritrea.
25. An Arabic word which translates as 'never mind'.
26. George Santayana: 'Oh World Thou Choosest Not'.
27. HMHS *Karapara* was built in 1914 and became a hospital ship for the second time in 1940 with 338 beds and 123 medical staff, serving between the Red Sea and India. On her second voyage she was bombed and set fire to at Tobruk, towed back to port, repaired and successfully sailed to Alexandria from where Joyce joined her. The ship still required repairs during the next year.
28. The rest of this sentence is redacted with blue pencil.

29. In the margin is written 'Mona's Viennese Knight'.
30. By Phyllis Bentley.
31. Antony Beevor's account differs, suggesting some wartime propaganda which was promulgated to the army: 'On August 25th, Red Army troops and British forces from Iraq invaded neutral Iran, to secure its oil and ensure a supply route from the Persian Gulf to the Caucasus and Kazakhstan.' Antony Beevor, *The Second World War* (Weidenfeld and Nicolson, 2012), p. 221.
32. James Ellroy Flecker travelled widely in the Middle East in the consular service and was a very popular poet, who died at the age of 30. His poem 'The Old Ships' begins: 'I have seen old ships sail like swans asleep.'
33. P.B. Shelley: 'Ozymandias'.
34. Omar Khayyam: 'Ah, Moon of my Delight who know'st no wane,/ The Moon of Heav'n is rising once again:/How oft hereafter rising shall she look/Through this same Garden after me – in vain!'
35. Now Pune, in southern India.
36. An ancient Iranian people who lived in northern Iran up to 670 BC.
37. Henry Wadsworth Longfellow: 'Shall fold their tents, like the Arabs/And as silently steal away'.
38. *John O'London's* started in 1919 and ran until 1954. It was a popular literary journal with a circulation of 80,000 at its peak. *Horizon: A Review of Literature and the Arts* was founded by Cyril Connolly and ran until 1949 with a circulation of around 9,000.
39. A vehicle used to transport personnel and equipment or as a machine-gun platform.
40. John Lehmann started *New Writing* in 1936, and then it became *Penguin New Writing* which ran from 1940 to 1946. It was committed to publishing writing that was anti-fascist.
41. W.B. Yeats: 'When you are Old'.
42. Robert Burns: 'Man was made to Mourn'.
43. A small Arab coin.
44. Capital of Ceylon, now capital of Sri Lanka.
45. Now Jakarta, Indonesia.

46. A small unit of Indian currency.
47. Joyce sailed on February 8th 1937 on the *Mongolia* from Australia to the UK to visit friends and family in Wales, where she worked until the outbreak of war.
48. A small light armed warship.
49. The name of Indonesia before the Second World War.
50. Milton, *Paradise Lost*: 'Thick as autumnal leaves that strew the brooks/ In Vallombrosa where Etrurian shades/ High over-arch'd embower.'
51. Indians from the province of Madras.
52. A non-commissioned officer equivalent to a sergeant.
53. Sevastopol, Ukraine.
54. The Aleutians are volcanic islands in the northern Pacific Ocean.
55. 220 miles off Yemen.
56. In Libya.
57. By John Cowper Powys.
58. Anne Ridler, *A Little Book of Modern Verse*, 1941.
59. John Masefield: 'Sea Fever'.
60. A journey of 1,035 miles.
61. The Old Monastery, Calcutta.
62. A drug for treating malaria.
63. A journey of over 800 miles.
64. Khalil Gibran.
65. Actually the son was Aurangzeb.
66. A type of headdress.
67. The Welsh word for homesickness.
68. A play by Emlyn Williams.
69. 'Dafydd' is the Welsh form of 'David'.
70. German and Italian troops surrendered in north Africa in May.
71. The Bengal Entertainment Services Association, founded in 1939 to provide entertainment for the British troops.
72. Thomas Gray: 'Elegy Written in a Country Churchyard'.
73. Now Dhaka, Bangladesh – a distance of 207 miles.

INDEX

9 780750 962308